FLYING CHEESE

STORIES FROM AN ORDINARY LIFE

By Rebecca K. Grosenbach

ISBN 978-1480262775

Edited by Carol Rebell

Designed by Steve Learned (zignguy@yahoo.com)

Unless otherwise identified, all Scripture quotations are taken from the Holy Bible: New International Version, Copyright 1984.

To Hubby

Contents

Cast of Characters

Many of these essays tell stories from my life, and many of them include my husband, Doug, and our children, Abby, Kate, and Eric. In these stories, I don't always say "my husband, Doug," or "my son, Eric." Pretend like you already know them. By the end of the book, you will.

Also, the kids have always called Doug "Papa." Or "O Captain My Captain." A lot of families call the grandfather "Papa," but for us, Papa is "Dad."

I'm blessed beyond words to be able to call these people my family. And for me to be "beyond words" is saying something.

Flying Cheese

Twenty years ago or so, before we had children, Doug and I were doing some after-work grocery shopping. It was a cold, Illinois-winter day, and I remember being bundled up in my long coat, scarf, and ear muffs, even inside the store. My glasses fogged up from the change in temperature.

I grabbed a cart and my dear husband and I headed down the dairy aisle. We needed sandwich cheese, and my mathematician mate bent over the cooler to calculate which package offered the cheapest slice. Knowing he had that under control, I left him to go across the aisle to get a carton of milk.

About that time, Doug decided he needed to say his figures out loud in order to complete the calculation. He turned to the woman next to him, thinking it was me, and said, "This is 16 slices for $2.65,"—or whatever it was—and then he said, "You're not my wife." He stood up to locate the real Mrs. G and spotted me about 15 feet away.

"Becky," he called, at which point I dutifully raised my head and turned my face in his direction. Almost simultaneously with calling my name he launched a package of sandwich cheese, allegedly hoping it would land in the cart.

I didn't have time to raise my mittened hands to deflect the dairy projectile, so it hit me right between the eyes. It busted my glasses across the bridge of my nose so now they were dangling from my ears, held there by my ear muffs.

Trying really hard not to laugh, Doug came over to make sure I was okay. The woman he had addressed in the cheese section followed a step behind and said, "Are you okay, dear? I'm sorry I wasn't his wife." She wasn't the only one.

What words could have described my emotions at that moment? Livid? Humiliated? Considering the context maybe "curdled" would have worked. But within a couple more rows of shopping I started to laugh. I pictured myself with my glasses dangling from my ear muffs . . . I pictured myself at work the next day—one of those days when I had to make a presentation to a room full of board members—with my glasses taped together like a classic "nerd."

There's a popular saying, "When life hands you lemons, make lemonade." What can we say about cheese? "When stuff hits you in the face like a pound of cheese, tape up your glasses and keep rolling."

And keep laughing.

Yes, Jesus Loves Me

"Jesus loves me this I know . . . ."

Three-year-old Abby believed that. I can still hear her singing *Jesus Loves Me* through her tears, sitting alone on her bed one afternoon. She had smeared shoe polish on the carpet. Black shoe polish. On the beige carpet. She knew it was wrong to be playing in Papa's shoe polish, and she knew she'd be punished.

"Go sit on your bed, and I'll be down in few minutes," Doug told her calmly. (Good thing he dealt with this one. I was not calm.)

The waiting was terrible. As the tears streaked her face, Abby sang, "Jesus loves me this I know . . . ."

I had to smile. In the face of discipline, Abby relied on God's love for her. Hebrews 12:6 says, "The Lord disciplines those he loves . . . ." It may be difficult to endure, but the motivation behind God's correction—always—is love.

Another time, late at night, Abby walked into our room crying. We couldn't determine what caused the tears, so we let her climb into bed and snuggle next to Papa.

After a few minutes Doug told her, "Abby it's time to go back to your bed."

"Okay, Papa," she said quietly. After she climbed into her bed, we could hear her softly sing, "Jesus loves me this I know . . . ."

She sang through her tears again, but it was enough to calm her down and help her sleep. She knew like the psalmist, "By day the Lord directs his love, at night his song is with me—a prayer to the God of my life" (Psalm 42:8).

Abby sang the song again on a sunny, spring morning. We were watching *Sesame Street* when the phone rang. It was my mother.

"Becky," Mom said. "Your dad went home to be with the Lord a few minutes ago."

I hung up the phone, unable to breathe. I looked at Abby, my chest ready to burst. I managed to say, "Grandpa Odell died," and I collapsed into the couch, sobbing.

It was then Abby walked over, put her hand on my knee, and sang,

> *Jesus loves me this I know*
> *For the Bible tells me so.*
> *Little ones to Him belong*
> *They are weak, but he is strong.*
> *Yes, Jesus loves me,*
> *Yes, Jesus loves me,*
> *Yes, Jesus loves me,*
> *The Bible tells me so.*

In her own little way my daughter comforted me. She didn't know any of the platitudes some people offer at such a time. She only knew to remind me that even in my time of deepest grief, Jesus loves me.

Psalm 34:4 says, "God is close to the broken hearted." And some-times He uses curly haired little three-year-olds to remind us just how close He is.

Through discipline.

Through darkness.

Through death.

Yes, Jesus loves me.

Jesus Loves Me, Anna Bartlett Warner, tune and chorus by William Batcheldor Bradburg

"Pease?"

By the tender age of two, Kate had already learned the power of good manners. "Please" and "thank you" were well-used members of her vocabulary.

One day I stood washing dishes at the kitchen sink, listening to the radio, when little Kate came toddling into the room.

"My music?" Kate asked, wanting me to put one of her cassettes into the combination radio/tape player.

"No, Honey. We need to take turns playing our music, and it's Mommy's turn to listen to her music right now."

Then, remembering her manners, Kate cocked her head to one side and said, "Pe-e-e-ease." The lack of the letter "l" made it all the more endearing.

Figuring it was a good opportunity to teach her the value of sharing, I repeated, "No, Honey, it's Mommy's turn," and resumed washing my dishes.

With that, Kate (quite uncharacteristically I might add) took two steps back, bent over, ran forward, and planted a solid head bump to my back side. "Pease!" she demanded.

Trying not to laugh, I told her head bumping was not appropriate and would do nothing to convince me to play her music.

Kate huffed and then trotted away. I smiled down at the soapy water. Then it struck me. *Do I ever treat God that way?*

Do I go through life expecting God to give me what I want if I use "good manners," if I'm a good girl and do what I think He wants me to do? What if that doesn't work? Do I stamp my feet and raise my fist and demand He do things my way?

I doubt I express my disappointment with God as openly as a two-year-old expresses her displeasure with her parent's decisions. But I'm sure I don't respond to things as I should. I place unrealistic expectations on God without realizing it. And I know I want my own way.

Just as Kate has grown into a lovely, sweet-tempered young woman, I hope I'll continue to mature in my relationship with my Father and learn to accept His decisions with grace and good temper, rather than fist shaking and head bumping. Well, figurative head bumping, anyway.

Climbing the Gate

One day, when Eric was about two, he met me on the stairs as I came out of the bathroom.

"Yucky pill," Eric said.

Oh no! my mind screamed. *What pills? What has he gotten into?*

I turned the corner into the kitchen and had my answer. Eric had pushed a kitchen chair across the room, climbed onto the chair, then onto the counter, and opened the cupboard where I kept a bottle of Fever Few, an herb that is supposed to help prevent migraines. (Is it any wonder I suffered from headaches?) It was a new bottle. I'd only taken one.

He had emptied the bottle on the kitchen floor. But not only the pills. Oh, no. Also a box of baking soda, a bottle of ground cinnamon, and about a cup of flour. And just enough water to make it bubble.

It was a terrible mess, but my first priority was to find out if Fever Few was poisonous to toddlers.

"Hello, this is Poison Control, Dave speaking. How may I help you?"

"My two-year-old son just got into my bottle of Fever Few."

"What?"

"Fever Few. It's an herb. It's supposed to help prevent—oh, never mind."

"How many did he take?"

"I don't know! He didn't tell me!"

"Do you know how many pills were in the bottle?"

"Yes, it was a brand new bottle. I'd only taken one."

"Well, count how many are left in the bottle."

"There are none left in the bottle! They are on my kitchen floor in a foaming, bubbling volcano!"

"Well, see how many you can find. Count them up while I do some research on Fever Few. Set the phone down but don't hang up."

I had no choice but to dig through the goo and find the remaining green capsules. . . . 46, 47, 48 . . . that's all of them. The bottle came with 50 pills. Fifty minus the one I took. Forty-nine. Minus the 48 flour-covered pills now sitting in the bottle. One.

"Dave," I said, picking up the phone again, "my son only ate one pill."

"Good. From what I can determine he should be okay. Just keep an eye on him."

"Thanks, Dave."

"You're welcome. And consider finding a better place to store your pills."

(Yeah, thanks. I thought they were in a safe place!)

I knew I had to make some changes. One possibility was to never go to the bathroom when I was home alone with Eric. In lieu of that, I stored the pills in the bathroom, and always stacked the kitchen chairs on top of the kitchen table. Not upside down, with the backs hanging over the sides, but standing upright, like soldiers, on top of the table. Where Eric couldn't reach them.

I also made better use of our baby gates. When I needed to keep Eric out of the kitchen, I'd set the gate where Eric could play in his room or go downstairs to the family room. Lots of room to play. Plenty of room to play. What did he do? He stood at the gate and cried to be let over so he could play in the kitchen.

Granted, part of the reason he wanted over the gate was that I was in the kitchen. But seeing him struggling so hard to get where I didn't want him to go made me think of Adam and Eve. God gave them a beautiful garden home and told them they could eat the fruit from any tree except one. One tree! Plenty to eat, plenty of places to go. But they wanted what was forbidden.

Sin does look attractive at times. Hebrews 11:25 uses the phrase "the pleasures of sin" because sin is appealing. I often want what I cannot have. I don't always desire things that would be classified as sin, I just want something "better" than what I already have. A larger house, nicer furniture . . . Nothing sinful about nicer stuff, is there?

The sin is my discontent. How often the apostle Paul's words echo in my mind: "I have learned to be content whatever the circumstances. I know what it is to be in need, and I know what it is to have plenty. I have learned the secret of being content in any and every situation, whether well fed or hungry, whether living in plenty or in want. I can do everything through him who gives me strength" (Philippians 4:11-13).

I take two lessons away from these verses. First, Paul "learned" to be content. It's something that takes practice. But at the same time, Paul said the secret was to rely on the strength of God. You can do everything—even be content!

So, how do we tap into God's strength?

Perhaps there is a hint in what Nehemiah told the Israelites. The people were sad because of their obvious disobedience to God. So Nehemiah said, "Do not grieve, for the joy of the Lord is your strength" (Nehemiah 8:10).

When we find our joy in the Lord, it gives us strength!

The same idea is expressed in the beautiful verses of Habakkuk 3:17 and 18: "Though the fig tree does not bud and there are no grapes on the vines, though the olive crop fails and the fields produce no food, though there are no sheep in the pen and no cattle in the stalls, yet I will rejoice in the Lord, I will be joyful in God my Savior."

Habakkuk determined that no matter what his situation, he would rejoice in the Lord. Maybe this was Paul's secret. Perhaps he learned to rejoice in the Lord, draw on the strength that He provides, and experience contentment, no matter what.

Just as Eric has outgrown his tendency to climb on kitchen counters, spiritual maturity will enable me to find contentment in my present place and circumstances. And stop climbing the gate.

How I Lost 25 Pounds

I have a constant battle with my weight. I love to eat, and my weight creeps up on me now and then. I'm not severely over-weight, just a little soft around the middle. But I'm definitely heavier than what our society describes as beautiful. In fact, I thought I was too heavy in high school—and I only weighed 115 pounds!

Shortly after I was married, I joined Weight Watchers. I wanted to lose about 20 pounds—which I think was the minimum amount of weight a person had to have as a goal. Ironically, I weighed less before I went on WW than I do now. In fact, I realized recently that my total weight gain in my childbearing years was roughly equivalent to the combined birth weight of my three children. And, considering they all weighed more than eight pounds, that is a lot of baby fat.

The eating plan I followed on Weight Watchers was effective, well-balanced, and not difficult to follow. I revert to the basics of that plan when I need to drop a few. (Admittedly, if I ate that way all the time, I'd never have a weight problem. I haven't mastered that yet.) I limit myself to three servings of starchy stuff a day (including bread, potatoes, rice, pasta, peas, corn, and the like), eat two or three fruit servings a day, eat lots of vegetables, three servings of protein (four ounces of meat is a serving), and eliminate sugar. I'm not talking about a total sugar elimination; I still eat things like ketchup or salad dressing that have sugar in them. I'm talking about the good stuff—cookies, *Milky Way Dark*, *Krispie Kreme*. I eat a lot of artificial sweetener in things like *Crystal Light Peach Tea* and sugar free pudding. In fact, I often use pudding as my daily treat. I fix a package of pudding, eat one cup, and save the second cupful for the next day. Another great treat is frozen strawberries—one cup a day.

I eat lots of salad. Almost every day for lunch, and it is a major part of my dinner. Some days I eat salad for a mid-morning snack. Weird, I know.

So that is my weight loss plan. But the real key to any kind of weight loss is motivation. Not discipline, but motivation. Some people say, "I don't have the discipline to stick with a diet," but I beg to differ. We're all disciplined. For instance, we all brush our teeth every day (I trust), maybe several times a day. Why? Because we want minty fresh breath, we want to keep our teeth in our heads, we don't want to pay high dental bills—whatever. We have the discipline to brush our teeth every day because we're properly motivated.

The same idea applies to weight loss. For instance, when I was on WW way back when, I stuck to the program religiously. Why? Because I was paying $10.00 a week to be a WW member. There was no way I was going to waste $10.00 a week by not sticking with the program.

Quite often when I lose weight, I'm motivated by wanting to impress people. Pretty bad motivation, but that's what it comes down to. Maybe it's a reunion, or a special event, and I want to look good. How vain. There are lots of motivations I could choose—reducing my blood pressure, avoiding heart disease, setting a good example for my children—but so far it's just been my own vanity.

I lost 25 pounds one year, but I confess much of it has found its way back home. It must have dropped bread crumbs or something.

Mmmm, bread crumbs.

I know in the big scheme of things it doesn't really matter that I'm three-baby-weights heavier than I used to be. Nobody I really care about is going to love me any more or any less if I gain a few pounds—or lose a few pounds. But I feel better about myself when I keep my weight down. And I guess that's motivation enough.

Mom's Things

It's December 2, 2004. I started putting away my Thanksgiving decorations yesterday. I took down the simple wooden "Give Thanks" sign that used to hang above Mom's front door. I removed the ceramic pilgrims Mom painted in 1977. (I know she made them because she scratched her "J.O." and "'77" on the bottom.) I emptied the miniature turkey salt and pepper shakers that used to adorn Mom's buffet.

Many of the decorations in my home were in my mother's house a month ago. But then, most unexpectedly, Mom went to be with her Savior on November 1.

Doctors think she may have been sick a few days but didn't say anything to anyone. On Sunday, October 31, she went to her local pharmacist. He noticed sweat on Mom's brow and that she was slightly bent over, holding her stomach. He finally insisted on calling an ambulance.

It is believed Mom had some kind of blockage in her bowel. Her body filled with poisons and she simply couldn't fight it off. By noon Monday she was gone.

Mom's funeral was scheduled for Friday, but Doug, the children, and I left our home in Colorado early Tuesday morning to head to Boise. That way we had a few days to spend with my four sisters, help plan Mom's service, and begin to go through Mom's belongings.

On the long, quiet ride across Wyoming, I thought about the idea of dividing up Mother's things. I determined that there was nothing in her house that was more important to me than my relationship with my sisters. And besides, all the best things Mom had to give me I already possessed. She had given me home, love, family, faith . . . . She was not an overly affectionate, "lovey-dovey" kind of mother, but she was devoted to us. She sacrificed much for our well-being. She never gossiped, she worked hard, and, boy dandy, could she cook.

My sisters and I spent hours dividing up what we wanted to keep in the family, selecting a few trinkets for Mom's friends, and giving many things to charity. There was never a harsh word exchanged, in fact, we often said, "You take it," or "You should have that," or "Keep that for one of your children." Mother would have been proud.

So, today, as I pack away the pilgrims and the turkeys, I'm reminded that these ornaments are merely things—beautiful, sentimental things—and that the best things my mother gave me I carry in my heart.

Resurrection

In honor of my father-in-law, a career Navy man, let me share the story of the *USS California*.

She was an old ship, commissioned August 10, 1921. For 20 years, the *California* served as a flagship, first for the Pacific Fleet, then for the Battle Fleet. She was updated a couple times in those years, and then in 1940, she switched her base to a place called Pearl Harbor.

On December 7, 1941, she was moored at the southernmost berth of "Battleship Row" when the Japanese launched their aerial attack. Just after 8:00 a.m. a bomb fell from the sky and exploded below deck, setting off an anti-aircraft ammunition magazine, killing about 50 men. A second bomb ruptured her bow. Despite valiant efforts to keep her afloat, the in-rushing water could not be stopped, and the *California* settled into the mud with only her superstructure remaining above the surface. When the bombing stopped, 98 of her crew were lost and 61 wounded.

There she sat, for three months. Repairs were made underwater and on March 25, 1942, she was refloated. After more work, she departed under her own power for Puget Sound Navy Yard in

Bremerton, Washington, where major reconstruction took place.

In January 1944 she was fit for duty. She steamed back into the front lines of the Pacific theater of World War II, including some action with Japan. By the end of the war, she had received seven Battle Stars.

We can learn a lot from that old battleship:

▶ We can be "destroyed" in an instant. A sudden catastrophe can leave us feeling buried, useless, helpless.
▶ Even when we're sunk, we need not consider ourselves finished.
▶ Reconstruction has to start underwater—in the unseen places—before we can return to action.
▶ After tragedy comes new opportunity.
▶ It might take a lot of time and a lot of work to recover, but it's better than staying stuck in the mud.
▶ Even old boats can earn gold stars.

I Am Resolved

I am a big fan of New Year's resolutions. My list always includes things like weight loss, exercise, daily Bible reading—things that require discipline and other unpleasantries.

The year after my mother died, I was drawn to more serious topics for my resolutions. That same year we also said good bye to a couple much-loved uncles, and it's Uncle Elvin who got me thinking about resolutions.

Uncle Elvin was Doug's mother's brother. I didn't know Uncle Elvin very well until after Eric was born. Eric arrived on Elvin's birthday, and Uncle Elvin got a real kick out of having a birthday twin (so did Eric). He started sending Eric hilarious computer-generated cards, and he always included a bit of green in the card, if you know what I mean. And he didn't do it just for Eric; all three of our children received Uncle Elvin-made birthday cards with a bit of green tucked inside.

When Uncle Elvin passed away just before Christmas, I thought about how generous he had been. Not only with "the green" but with his time. It took real effort to make those cards for us every year. And I know we weren't the only ones to receive them, or the only ones to benefit from a "bit of the green."

The other uncle we said good bye to that fall was my Uncle Bill, the husband of my mother's only sister, Betty. Uncle Bill was a quiet, hard-working Iowa farmer. I don't know how he did it, but Uncle Bill made me feel special. I can remember him inviting me up on his knee when I was little. He taught me how to whistle like a bird. He gave me—the littlest member of the family— his undivided attention. Uncle Bill had a knack for focusing his attention on other people rather than trying to attract attention to himself.

So, as I made my New Year's resolutions, I decided to honor these loved ones by emulating some of their best qualities. For Mom, I resolved to be more organized. For Uncle Elvin, I decided to be more generous. And for Uncle Bill, I tried to focus more on other people and less on myself.

Of course, the ultimate Loved One I should emulate is Christ. Just think of the qualities I'd have on my list if I chose to be like Jesus. As the old hymn says:

> *Earthly pleasures vainly call me, I would be like Jesus.*
> *Nothing worldly shall enthrall me, I would be like Jesus.*
> *Be like Jesus, this my song, In the home and in the throng;*
> *Be like Jesus, all day long! I would be like Jesus.*

I Would Be Like Jesus, by James Rowe and Bentley D. Ackley, Hope Publishing, © 1912, 1940

Eric Is Nine

My son turned nine yesterday. In case you're not aware, nine is painfully close to 10. And 10 is just inches away from 13. Which, as anyone knows, is in the same category as 18. That means my son is nearly ready to look at college brochures, move out of the house, and—well, maybe I'm overreacting. But I'm having a hard time accepting the fact that this is the last year someone in our house will be a single digit old.

Eric is such fun to have around. Sunday we were at the home of some good friends watching the Broncos game on TV. (I've been told the Broncos are a football team of some note. I'm really only interested in the Chicago Bears. Old loyalties die hard.) The game was interrupted by a commercial for *60 Minutes*, the long-running news magazine show. They showed a clip from an interview of some famous person—I didn't know who he was—who had a "thousand-dollar-a-day cocaine habit."

My son, only giving the commercial half his attention, turned to me and asked, "What was that? A thousand dollars a day on croquet?"

It took me a minute to respond to him because I was seized with laughter. The silent, tears-rolling-down-your-face laughter that made it impossible to breathe, let alone form sentences.

But, as funny as it was, I was also relieved that the word "cocaine" didn't register in his brain. All too soon his innocence will be spent. He'll know exactly what's being talked about. In fact, he already knows about smoking and drugs to a certain degree. His school is very good about having an annual "red ribbon week" where they teach the children to abstain from drugs and smoking. I'm glad they give him such education, but I'm sorry he needs it.

He's a whole lot closer to 18 than I want to admit. But, for now, I'll relish his nine-year-old hugs, his third-grade enthusiasm, and the fact that he still wants me to tuck him into bed at night.

I just realized nine is exactly half of 18. He's halfway through his growing up years. Before you know it, he'll be driving, and then getting his first job, and . . . .

Silver and Gold

"Dear Friends . . . . "

It's a common salutation, but it's also a description of one of life's greatest gifts, a treasure I came to appreciate anew when my mother died.

I received cards from friends in Iowa, Oregon, Washington, Illinois. Friends from childhood, friends from high school, friends from our "just married" days. Some of them shared memories of Mom or of our growing up years. Others said things like, "I lost my mother three years ago and I still miss her." It helps to know they understand.

I e-mailed a friend whose mother died several years ago. I told her, "Sometimes I'll think, 'I need to tell Mom—' and then catch myself, realizing I can't tell Mom." My friend told me, "I decided that when I think of something I would want to tell Mom, I just go ahead and tell her." I do that now, too. It helps.

Friends here in town brought me flowers, made us dinner, gave hugs. They'd ask how I was doing and really listen to my answer.

The Girl Scouts sing, "Make new friends, but keep the old. One is silver and the other gold." If that be true, I'm richer than I deserve.

Here are some lines that express my thoughts perfectly.

A Friend's Greeting
by Edgar A.Guest

I'd like to be the sort of friend that you have been to me;
I'd like to be the help that you've been always glad to be;
I'd like to mean as much to you each minute of the day
As you have meant, old friend of mine, to me along the way.

I'd like to do the big things and the splendid things for you,
To brush the gray from out your skies and leave them only blue;
I'd like to say the kindly things that I so oft have heard,
And feel that I could rouse your soul the way that mine you've
*   stirred.*

I'd like to give you back the joy that you have given me,
Yet that were wishing you a need I hope will never be;
I'd like to make you feel as rich as I, who travel on
Undaunted in the darkest hours with you to lean upon.

I'm wishing at this Christmas time that I could but repay
A portion of the gladness that you've strewn along my way;
And could I have one wish this year, this only would it be;
I'd like to be the sort of friend that you have been to me.

The Best Loved Poems of the American People, Hazel Felleman, editor, Double-day, New York, NY, 1936.

My "Ah-Ha" Moment

I am fortunate to live and work near one of the most beautiful spots on the planet: Garden of the Gods. This registered National Natural Landmark on the west edge of Colorado Springs is punctuated with huge, jagged, terra cotta rock formations, sandstone cliffs, green pines. Opposite the Garden and up another ridge is a scenic overlook, a small parking lot created to give a picture perfect view of the park and Pikes Peak in the background. Whenever I drive by that spot, I'm reminded of an "ah-ha" moment I had there years ago.

My place of employment neighbors the park, and when I first started working there, I worked part-time. It fit perfectly in my schedule. At the time, I drove Kate to and from middle school, and my working hours nestled sweetly in the middle of the day, allowing me to operate my taxi service.

One day, I had an extra fare in my morning route—I had to take Abby to school, too. Because this required me to leave home earlier than usual, I wasn't quite ready when the clock told me it was time to go. I hadn't put on my make up, so I decided to take it with me and find a place to "put on my face" before I arrived at work. There were any number of parking lots I could pull into on my way.

So, after dropping off my darlings, I started on towards work. I decided I would stop on Mesa Road at the scenic overlook.

I pulled into the small parking area, turned off the car, flipped down the visor, and opened the mirror. I unzipped my make up bag and pulled out the under eye concealer and applicator sponge. I looked at my face in the mirror and it happened. The "ah-ha" moment.

I thought, *Becky, do you realize what is on the other side of that visor?* I knew, of course. It's the stuff of which postcards are made. As if to remind myself, I put the visor up and looked. Sure enough, there it was. Breathtaking. And there I sat, looking at my ugly mug in a mirror.

The "ah-ha" part was this: I was concentrating on me, on my flaws, on the stuff that was up close, when right there in front of me was one of the most beautiful things in all Creation. How often in life do I miss the beauty around me because I'm preoccupied with "me"?

Ah-ha . . . .

Like, Groovy

"Mom, have you ever heard of capris?"

Abby asked me this a while back when the short pants came back into style. I suppressed a laugh and told her, yes, I had heard of them. After all, I'd seen *The Dick Van Dyke Show*. Laura Petrie wore capris quite often and looked smashing in them.

I told Abby we used to call them "pedal pushers."

"Ha! Pedal pushers. That's a good one," she mocked.

As other '60s and '70s styles came back into fashion. I had to relearn the proper names for things. What used to be "bell bottoms" are now "flairs." "Hip huggers" have become "low risers."

The really serious offense is when I refer to the rubber sandal-like footwear as "thongs." I know, I know, the word has come to refer to a certain style of undergarments and I should call the sandals "flip flops," which is a much better name, aptly describing the annoying, incessant slapping of the shoe on the foot. I still slip every once in a while (old habits die hard), to the extreme embarrassment of my children.

Abby introduced me to another new word one summer when we went to pick her up from camp. As we joined her in the chapel for a closing video, she turned me to me and said, "I want to sit with my peeps."

Now, I looked around the room rather carefully, and I never found any small, marshmallow birds. Then I a saw her sit with her friends. Apparently, her friends are "peeps."

When she returned I pressed her for an interpretation. "People," she said. "I wanted to sit with my people, my peeps."

The other day in the car, Eric laid one on me. He was trying to explain something to me and finally said, "You get my flow," which, given the context, I took to mean, "You get my drift."

The most annoying language quirk of my children's generation (although it has been around much longer) is the use of the word "like" as an interrupter, an "um" or an "uh."

While I might say, "Kate, you look nice in that shirt," Kate's friends might say, "Like, Kate, you look, like, nice in that, like, shirt."

Well, I'm sure my parents shook their heads when I said "groovy" or "far out." And I'd rather, like, put up with my children's, like, odd vocabulary than, like, not talk at all.

Right on? Right on.

Thanks for Coming

Babies. Ya gotta love 'em.

Literally. You have to love them. They're too cute not to love. I remember reading the results of a research project conducted by a psychologist (who no doubt received grant money to complete the study) about what physical features people think are most attractive. The study revealed that large eyes are what most people identify as "cute." Which is why, the psychologist concluded, we find babies cute. Our eyes do not grow—they are the same size when we're born as when we die—so they are disproportionately large as babies. So we think babies are cute. (Large eyes also explain why movie goers found the character E.T. cute, even though he was a wrinkled, flat-headed alien.)

I think most people will agree with me that there is more to love in a newborn than just her large eyes. There is the fuzzy head, the chubby legs, the perfect little ears. And just the fact that she's "yours" makes you love her in a way you never thought possible.

But I digress. Babies. One summer, within the span of a month, our family welcomed three new babies, born to three of our beautiful nieces. Susan Grace was born to Laurie and Dan (their second daughter). Emma Jeane was born to Amy and Steve (their first child). And Benjamin Oliver was born to Rebekah and Adam (their second son).

Unfortunately, none of these little wonders lived within snuggling distance. But when I did get to see them, I'd hug them close and whisper, "Thank you for coming." Each of them brings such promise, such hope, such delight. And we need that kind of thing nowadays.

These children arrived at the same time that Hurricane Katrina ravaged the southeastern United States. I watched news coverage of comedian Chris Rock visiting some of the displaced families. He was overcome by the plight of the people he encountered. He made a statement something like, "All we have is family. We think we have houses and belongings, but they can all be gone in a moment. All we have is family."

I might change his statement a bit to include our friends. So maybe we could say, "All we have is people." Most of us have had—or will have at some point in our lives—experiences that teach us that our stuff, our jobs, or whatever else we may value, are not nearly as important as people.

I think the new babies remind me of that. Susan, Emma, and Benjamin remind me that the most precious things in life aren't things, it's the people we love.

So, "thanks for coming."

Don't Touch That Dial!

When Eric was in third grade, he wanted to participate in a school program called "Read Across America." This program encourages families to turn off the television and read together. Eric's school sent home a flyer indicating three things we needed to do for Eric to qualify for a special luncheon. First, no television or video games Monday through Friday. Second, read as a family for 30 minutes each day. And third, complete a book-related project, such as making a book mark or writing a summary.

To provide incentive for the rest of us, Doug offered to take us out for dinner on Sunday. So we all agreed to go five days without TV.

Now, it's not like TV is a necessity. We can easily live without it. But I'm surprised at how often we click on the TV almost without thinking. The kids come home from school and watch TV to unwind. Doug and I often crawl into bed and watch an episode of *M*A*S*H* before going to sleep.

But that week was different. Eric and Kate played outside after school. Eric and I played a couple hands of the card game "Upstairs Downstairs" when we had a few minutes. I read the newspaper. And Doug and I talked before going to sleep instead of watching Hawkeye and the gang. Abby said it just made her cranky.

As instructed, we read 30 minutes every day. A couple days we had to read over dinner because that was the only 30 minutes we were all together. We read *The Lion, the Witch, and the Wardrobe,* the first book in C.S. Lewis' Chronicles of Narnia. We love the book (which we'd all read before), and we enjoyed reading aloud to each other.

After a few days, I asked my family, "Would you like to make long-term changes to our viewing habits?"

The family seemed open to the idea. I told them about some friends from church who limit their TV viewing to an hour a day. We have other friends who never watch TV, only the occasional movie. Nobody suggested we go without television altogether, but maybe I should have. After all, it's not like TV is a necessity. We can easily live without it. Or so I've been told.

Prayer Changes Things— Or Does It?

One winter, our pastor used his Sunday evening sermons to answer questions posed by the congregation. These questions were submitted in writing so Pastor had time to prepare a response.

One Sunday, he answered my question. Folks didn't know it was my question. Pastor Lance didn't identify who wrote the questions, but I'll identify it: It was mine.

It was a rather wordy, long-winded question (imagine that), but basically the issue was, "Why pray when God knows/determines the future anyway?"

Our pastor raised a number of good points. First of all, we pray because God has instructed us to do so. Philippians 4:6 says, ". . . let your requests be made known to God."

Also, Jesus prayed, and since He did, we should too. Matthew 14:23 says, ". . . He [Jesus] went up to the mountain by Himself to pray . . . ."

Answered prayer glorifies God: "And whatever you ask in My

name, that will I do, that the Father may be glorified in the Son" (John 14:13).

Prayer is powerful and effective. You can probably quote James 5:16: "The effective prayer of a righteous man can accomplish much." James also says, "You do not have because you do not ask" (James 4:2).

The next point Pastor made was a real light bulb moment for me. In Ezekiel 36, beginning at verse 22, God tells the children of Israel all the kind things He was going to do for them. He says He is going to bring them into their own land, "sprinkle clean water on them" so they will be clean. He promises them a new heart and a new spirit. The Israelites would see God "multiply the fruit of the tree."

God obviously has a plan in mind here. Then, in verse 37, He says, "This also I will let the house of Israel ask Me to do for them; I will increase their men like a flock." It's as if God is saying, "I intend to bless you, but I'm going to let you ask me for it." God allows us to participate in His work through prayer. Not that our prayers change God's plan; our prayers are part of the plan.

"Prayer is God's foreordained path to fulfilling His foreordained plans that accomplish His foreordained purposes," Pastor said.

Yes, God has the future all worked out, but somehow our prayers are part of the equation. Prayer is a great mystery and a great privilege.

And that's why we pray.

Of Slide Rules
and Calculators

It was bound to happen eventually: I became the mother of a high schooler. It's a condition that has lasted for several years.

As Abby's freshman year dawned, she was told she should get some highfalutin calculator. A special "graphing calculator" made by Texas Instruments. We went to Target to get one. I looked at the price tag and burst out, "A hundred dollars?!" And burst is not an overstatement. I clapped my hand over my mouth and repeated, "A hnded dllrs?"

I refused to purchase a hundred-dollar calculator.

We discussed it over dinner that evening.

"But Mom," she protested, "my teacher says I will have to have one next year, so why not go ahead and get it now?"

"Well," I responded calmly, "I'm not convinced you need it. Your father was a math *major* in college, and I dare say graphing calculators didn't even exist then. He did the same calculations using paper and pencil."

"And a slide rule," her father added. "I'll bet your teacher doesn't have a six foot long slide rule."

"A what?" Abby asked.

"Precisely!" I responded. "People are able to do complex equations without the help of 'graphing calculators.' In fact, when I was in high school [a phrase that causes Abby's eyes to roll back into her head] it was considered cheating to use calculators."

"Well, I can't help it if your teachers were, . . . um . . .," she paused, searching for the right word, "if they were Quakers or something."

Quakers—her word for people who compute mathematical equations without calculators.

I was expecting a little more help from my mathematician husband, but to my surprise he was at least open to the idea of purchasing a $100 calculator.

"What if we considered it my calculator and you can use it?" he suggested. I'm not sure how that changed anything. Maybe he just wanted to be able to say he owned a graphing calculator *and* a slide rule.

"Let's get on the Internet and compare prices," he suggested. One store listed the price at $79.99. Funny how that sounded like a bargain.

As you might predict, Abby got her graphing calculator. I wonder what she'll be complaining about when her daughter starts high school.

"A neuro-holographic generator? For two hundred dollars? Er— tw hmmnd dllrs? No way! Back when I was in high school . . . ."

I Will Lift Up My Eyes

Several years ago, as I drove to work, a fog hung over Colorado Springs. I couldn't see Pikes Peak—the sheltering mountain that borders the west side of town. It was as if someone had pulled a curtain across the foothills. I felt like I was in an entirely different place. I knew the mountains were still there, of course, but I sure couldn't see them.

As I drove closer to the mountains, though, the familiar images began to emerge. The jagged ridges, the red clay ground, the green pines. And by the time I left work at mid-day the sun had returned everything to normal.

How like our spiritual lives. Sometimes our circumstances seem to draw a veil between us and God. The clouds of disappointment or sorrow make it more difficult to see Him. But rather than assume He's not there, we need to draw closer to Him. Step nearer God when times are hard and His face will break through. James 4:8 reminds us, "Draw near to God, and He will draw near to you."

Just as the mountains were unmoved, so our God is unchanging, ever faithful, ever true. That is the definition of faith, my friend.

Believing that God is still God, even when we don't understand our circumstances. The things that are true of God in the "daylight" are equally true in the "darkness." God is love (1 John 4). God is light (1 John 1).

These truths have helped me through many dark days, like a lighthouse guiding me through rough seas, reminding me of the shoreline:

"The Lord is near to the brokenhearted, and saves those who are crushed in spirit" (Psalm 34:18).

"God is our refuge and strength, a very present help in trouble" (Psalm 46:1).

"As the mountains surround Jerusalem, so the Lord surrounds His people from this time forth and forever" (Psalm 125:2).

"Casting all your anxiety upon Him because He cares for you" (1 Peter 5:7).

"After you have suffered for a little while, the God of all grace, who called you to His eternal glory in Christ, will Himself perfect, confirm, strengthen, and establish you" (1 Peter 5:10).

"I will lift up my eyes to the mountains: From whence shall my help come? My help comes from the Lord, who made heaven and earth" (Psalm 121:1,2).

All I Really Need to Know
I Learned from
a Ten-Year-Old

One summer day, when Kate's and Eric's ages averaged 10, I had occasion to spend a day with them. No Doug, no Abby, just me and "the kids." I learned a lot from them; allow me to enlighten you.

- Bike riding is fun. Skating is fun. But riding a bike with skates on is even more fun.
- A piece of fiberboard propped up on one end by a bag of sand makes a nice skating ramp.
- However, the same piece of fiberboard balanced in the center on a bag of sand makes a poor teeter-totter.
- Newly remodeled McDonald's restaurants with video games decrease a boy's appetite by 50 percent.
- One sure remedy for an upset stomach is a loud, prolonged belch. ("Ahhh, I feel much better now.")
- The more a child asks "can we go yet," the longer it takes a mother to finish the yard work.

- The more a child helps a mother with the yard work the sooner "we can go." (Strange how this lesson was abundantly clear to me and not so clear to the other people present.)
- Large, plastic, garbage bags, when released carefully into a slight breeze, can fly several feet, though it is difficult to repeat the maneuver, even with numerous attempts.
- It is impossible to fill large, plastic, garbage bags with yard waste when the bags are being flight tested.
- Girls prefer to change clothes between yard work and miniature golfing.
- Boys are not aware of the need to change clothes between yard work and miniature golfing.
- The pleasure experienced at a miniature golf course is in direct proportion to the number of water hazards encountered.
- When a 40-something woman encounters trouble remembering the entree numbers from the Vietnamese restaurant menu, an accompanying 11-year-old girl is able to recall the numbers without opening the menu.

The most important lesson I learned is that I genuinely enjoy my children, and I need to be sure we spend more time together, working, playing, and belching.

Ahhh, I feel much better now.

I Wish I'd Said That

On the way home from work the other day, someone on the radio quoted Harry Truman, saying, "It is amazing what you can accomplish if you do not care who gets the credit." I liked the quote, and decided to confirm it online. While I was there, I jotted down a few other gems.

- Happiness is not a goal; it is a by-product.—*Eleanor Roosevelt*
- Children are apt to live up to what you believe of them.—*Lady Bird Johnson*
- Associate yourself with men of good quality if you esteem your own reputation. It is better to be alone than in bad company.—*George Washington*
- I feel that luck is preparation meeting opportunity.—*Oprah Winfrey*
- Housework, if you do it right, will kill you.—*Erma Bombeck*
- Great minds discuss ideas; average minds discuss events; small minds discuss people.—*Eleanor Roosevelt*
- It is impossible to rightly govern a nation without God and the Bible.—*George Washington*
- Writing is hard work and bad for the health.—*E. B. White*

- Afflictions are but the shadows of God's wings.—*George Mac-Donald*
- There are two kinds of people: those who say to God, "Thy will be done," and those to whom God says, "All right, then, have it your way."—*C. S. Lewis*
- No one can make you feel inferior without your consent. —*Eleanor Roosevelt*
- There is no other way of writing a novel than to begin at the beginning and to continue to the end.—*C. S. Forester*
- My second favorite household chore is ironing. My first being hitting my head on the top bunk bed until I faint.—*Erma Bombeck*
- You don't have a soul. You are a Soul. You have a body.—*C.S. Lewis*

It would be nice if these quotes were all from people whose character I respected. But I still like what they had to say. As my friend Tim says, "Even a blind squirrel finds a nut once in a while."

And you may quote him on that.

Man's Best Friend

I love dogs.

I love their uninhibited affection for their masters. I remember the little dog we had when I was growing up—Pebbles. I know, it's a geeky name, but she was already named when we picked her out from among her brothers and sisters. And a few years later, when I discovered my new best friend had a cat named Bam Bam, I decided it was an okay name.

Anyway, Pebbles was a yappy Chihuahua mix, and she disliked strangers. But, for her family, she was full of affection. Especially for Dad. He'd walk in the front door after work and Pebbles would start this little welcome home dance. She wagged her tail, lifted her front legs, pawing the air, and then bowed down low to the ground—the tail going the whole time. She was perpetual wiggle.

Now, if I, as my father's daughter, had done some kind of welcome home dance, I'd be thought strange. But dogs can get away with it. They can show all the delight in the world at the sight of their masters. It's a wonderful thing.

I love their zest for life. Consider a dog in a moving car. What is it with the head out the window thing? I've heard that the dog is trying to take in all the smells in the air. But I think the dog is just enjoying the moment. Maybe he loves the feeling of his ears flapping in the wind. He gets that sense of flying without having to leave the ground.

I also love the way a dog has no self-awareness. Have you seen a poodle in a dog show? Their hair is poofed in spots, shaved in other spots. If he had any idea how ridiculous he looked, he wear a trench coat. But no—he struts around with all the other hounds thinking he's the pick of the litter. Dogs can be dyed, blow dried, dressed, bedecked, and bejeweled and they don't care. They just don't care. I get self-conscious when my hair gets a little frizzy.

You've likely heard the joke about the difference between dogs and cats. A dog says, "You feed me, you play with me, you clean up after me—you must be a god!" A cat says, "You feed me, you play with me, you clean up after me—I must be a god!"

Yeah, I prefer dogs. I wish I were as free in my expression of affection, as ready to seize the day, as unaware of my own self. So if you see me do a happy-to-see-you-dance sometimes, just pat me on the head and tell me I'm a good girl, and understand that I'm trying to be a little more like man's best friend.

Biker Dudes

I discovered something rather unpleasant about myself one summer afternoon. I'm a bigot. Well, maybe "bigot" is a little strong. I asked my dictionary for a definition and it said a bigot is "a narrow minded and intolerant person." Perhaps I am just "prejudiced," having "an opinion against something without adequate basis." Allow me to elucidate—uh, sorry. I had that dictionary thing going. Allow me to "do some 'splainin.'"

One Saturday afternoon when Eric was around nine, he was beg—er—asking me repeatedly with great urgency to take him to a skate park, one of those concrete havens of skaters and skateboarders. I finally agreed to take Eric and his rollerblades "somewhere" when I took Abby to her dance class one afternoon.

I asked Abby if kids skated at her former school, which is near the dance studio. She told me kids rode bikes there, but she didn't know about skates. Nonetheless, this was one place we checked after dropping off Abby for her jigs and reels.

Sure enough, as Abby predicted, there were some kids on bikes. On closer observation, I realized these weren't middle schoolers, these were older guys, maybe late teens, early twenties.

Eric and I stood on the side and watched for a minute when one of the young men said, "It's okay if he wants to skate here. He won't be in our way."

How nice, I thought. Actually, I thought something more like, *Wow, he's nice. And he's not a hood or a mugger or anything.*

Eric donned his skates and pads and started crisscrossing the pavement. Actually, he spent more time watching the biker dudes. They were pretty impressive.

Later, the biker dudes rode around the school to check out other challenges. Soon, Eric was ready to follow. That side of the school had a courtyard, brick planters, and a ramp. Again, Eric skated a bit, but found himself doing more watching than skating.

After several minutes he took off his skates altogether and sat down next to me on one of the aforementioned brick planters. By that time, the biker dudes were taking a break, and I encouraged Eric to go over and strike up a conversation with them. "Ask them about their bikes," I prompted.

Eric walked over and asked, "What's so special about your bikes?"

One young man gave a very detailed response, explaining why the bikes had no seat, the importance of strong brakes and rubbery tires. He even pointed to one of his friends and said, "This guy's really good. I'm just a beginner." What's that? Humility?

Yes, I was a biker bigot. I assumed young men on trick bikes were trouble makers and ne'er-do-gooders. But my prejudices were blown out of the water by a group of kind, friendly, articulate, and humble young men.

Right on, dudes.

Lyman, Wyoming

The year 2007 started off with a bang. And a crash. Our family was involved in a car accident while returning to Colorado after a vacation in Idaho. Icy roads resulted in the side of our minivan getting up close and personal with the rear corner of a semi truck trailer. The worst injury was a bad cut on Abby's right ring finger, which required stitches.

I'll spare you the other accident details, except to say that we wouldn't be able to make the rest of the trip in our van. The chief of police drove me and the kids to Lyman, Wyoming, because that was the nearest town with a place Abby could get the stitches she needed. Doug followed in the van—and nearly froze to death in the process. The side door had been removed by the jaws of life.

What we didn't realize was Lyman has no car-rental companies and no other viable alternatives for stranded motorists. After several phone calls, we accepted an offer from friends in Colorado Springs to drive up to Lyman and retrieve us and our van. However, our friends—both named Bob—couldn't come right away. It turned out it was just as well they waited. The weather remained ugly for a few days.

We settled into a small motel room and counted our blessings.

I think we all realized there was nothing we could do to change our situation and we tried to make the best of it. Lyman didn't offer much in the way of diversions. The town had no grocery store (but it did have a snowmobile dealership). There was a post office and a drug store. The theater showed one movie once a day (twice on Saturday). Next to the motel was a Laundromat.

Two doors down was the Branding Iron Café. It was one of those classic country restaurants with great food and generous portions—and the best onion rings on the planet. We would go for lunch and bring half of it back to the motel room for dinner (there was a mini fridge and a microwave in our room).

Most of the time it was too cold to be outside, so we hung out in our motel room. We had cable TV and saw reruns of some of our favorite shows. There was a children's game show Abby used to enjoy when she was in grade school with a temple maze and talking statue. All three of the kids watched it with great enthusiasm. Doug and I enjoyed old shows like The Avengers, The Wild, Wild, West, and Kung Fu.

I finished the book my mother-in-law loaned me. We played a few rounds of Zilch, a dice game. And we discovered we had internet access. Kate and Eric—and my laptop—enjoyed long hours of some game with digging and mining for treasure.

We discovered nice people. People in the Branding Iron, where we went upon first arriving in town, helped us contact a doctor for Abby. The doctor made a special trip into town and opened the clinic to stitch up Abby's finger. Folks tried to help us get to a larger town where we might have more options. "Jimmy owns the towing service across the street. Give him a call," one man said.

At Taco Time we saw one of the emergency workers who helped us after our collision. I didn't recognize him, but he made a point of introducing himself and asking how we were getting along.

Of course, nice people like we met in Lyman aren't unique to small towns. After all, it was a couple of city dwellers who drove hundreds of miles over two days to bring us home. And they weren't the only ones to extend the offer.

While it wouldn't have been on my list of "Top Ten Ways to Bring in a New Year," spending a few days in Lyman altered my New Year's resolutions. I realized I wanted to put a greater emphasis on people. I wanted to have our friends over more often. I wanted to be nicer to strangers. I wanted to go out of my way to help people. And eat more onion rings.

Doxology

I remember singing the Doxology every Sunday in church as a little girl. I also remember the day I realized I was actually singing English words, not some obscure form of Baptist Latin. "Pay gah fum who al bleh sing fo . . ." suddenly translated into "Praise God from whom all blessings flow."

I don't think the Doxology is sung as much as it used to be, but I sang it several times during a trip to Idaho. We were visiting relatives, part of the time in Boise with my side of the family, and part of the time in Caldwell with the Grosenbach clan. More than once, Dad G. had us sing the Doxology as we sat down to eat. The harmonies provided by Doug, his parents, sister, and my own humble alto were heavenly. And the words—the English words— are beautiful, too. Praise . . . praise . . . praise . . . .

While it doesn't rhyme or fit with a tune, I thought of my own doxology during that visit.

Praise God for my family. It's still kind of strange to go to Boise and not see my parents. They've both passed away. But my sisters, nieces, and nephews made up for any sadness I felt. As did Captain Gaseous, Burpazoid, and their side kick, Belch Boy.

In Caldwell, we attended the Tish Family Picnic, a July tradition for some 50 years. My grandmother-in-law was a Tish cousin, so I guess we are, too. I relished listening to some of the elder Tishes tell me of their loves and losses.

Praise God for music. One afternoon, Doug's sisters Norma and Marla sat in the bedroom and played French horn duets. Later in the week, Dad brought out his baritone and the cutest E-flat horn and he and Doug played together. Mom's magic fingers on the piano tied it all together. Norma told me that much of her early theology was based on hymns. If it included the Doxology—the English words—she was off to a good start.

Praise God for faithful servants. We sang the Doxology in Mom and Dad's church Sunday, the church Doug attended when he lived in Caldwell. The church full of friends, relatives, and familiarity. The pastor of the church performed our wedding ceremony in 1981. He has seen our extended family through happy occasions, too many sad ones, and all the days in between.

Just before we hit the road for the long drive back to Colorado Monday morning, we stood in a circle with Mom, Dad, and Norma, held bands and sang.

> *Praise God from whom all blessings flow.*
> *Praise Him all creatures here below.*
> *Praise Him above ye heavenly host.*
> *Praise Father, Son, and Holy Ghost.*
> *Amen.*

Amen, indeed.

Praise God from Whom All Blessings Flow, Words by Thomas Ken, 1674. Music from Old 100th, Genevan Psalter, attributed to Louis Bourgeois, 1551.

Still Bravely Singing

In recent years, I have come to love a poem entitled In Flanders Fields. The poem was written by John McCrae, a Canadian physician. When World War I broke out, McCrae was sent to Belgium as a field surgeon. He was in charge of a field hospital during the Second Battle of Ypres [e-pray] in 1915. McCrae's friend Alexis Helmer was killed in the battle, and his burial inspired the poem. In 1918, while still serving in the field hospital, McCrae caught pneumonia and meningitis and died.

Flanders is a region in northern Belgium. The poppies referred to in the poem grew in profusion in the fields where war casualties had been buried. Poppies have since become a symbol of remembrance for fallen soldiers. The poem reads:

> In Flanders fields the poppies blow
> Between the crosses, row on row,
>   That mark our place; and in the sky
>   The larks, still bravely singing, fly
> Scarce heard amid the guns below.

We are the Dead. Short days ago
We lived, felt dawn, saw sunset glow,
 Loved, and were loved, and now we lie
 In Flanders fields.

Take up our quarrel with the foe:
To you from failing hands we throw
 The torch; be yours to hold it high.
 If ye break faith with us who die
We shall not sleep, though poppies grow
In Flanders fields.

The Best Loved Poems of the American People includes *In Flanders Fields* and a few poems written "in reply" to Dr. McCrae. One of them is *America's Answer* by R.W. Lilliard.

Rest ye in peace, ye Flanders dead.
The fight that ye so bravely led
We've taken up. And we will keep
True faith with you who lie asleep
With each a cross to mark his bed,
 In Flanders fields.

Fear not that ye have died for naught.
The torch ye threw to us we caught.
Ten million hands will hold it high,
And Freedom's light shall never die!
We've learned the lesson that ye taught
 In Flanders fields.

The Best Loved Poems of the American People, Hazel Felleman, editor, Doubleday, New York, NY, 1936.

Better than
Reader's Digest

You know how it is on long road trips. Wa-a-a-a-y too much time on your hands.

For example, our family took a trip through the Northwest one summer. On a picturesque stretch of road across Washington, we—somehow—started coming up with puns on the term "basso profundo," a person who sings the lowest of the low notes. At the time, we thought they were very funny. But, then again, we'd been in the car a long time.

Here's our list:

- ► A bass who spends too much time playing video games: basso Nintendo
- ► A tenor who tries to sing bass: basso pretendo
- ► A bass we could really do without: basso expendo
- ► A bass who loves to argue: basso contendo
- ► A bass who belongs in therapy: basso dimento
- ► A bass who left his heart in California: basso San Francisco
- ► A bass who has caffeine jitters: basso espresso

- A bass from the Lone Star State: basso remember the Alamo
- A bass who loves his chips: basso Dorito
- A bass who is also a home run king: basso Bambino
- A bass who sings louder and louder and louder: basso crescendo
- A bass with serious bad breath: basso needs a Mento

When we returned from our trip, I sent the list to *Reader's Digest*. I thought they'd stop the presses, publish it in their next issue with an announcement about how to obtain reprints of the article. Such brilliant humor!

Guess what? Yeah, you're right. They didn't buy it.

That's okay. We have the memory of riding down the road, scribbling our ideas on the back of an envelope, laughing our fool heads off. I tell you, the tears rolled down my cheeks when Abby came up with "basso needs a Mento." Memories—that's something *Reader's Digest* can't buy!

Just Another Street Musician

If you had the opportunity to hear one of the world's most gifted, charismatic classical musicians play some of the world's greatest music—for free—would you take advantage of it?

More than 1,000 people had such an opportunity in Washington, D.C.,, back in 2007, but very few took advantage of it. To be fair, they didn't realize they were being offered such a rare opportunity, but they dismissed it just the same.

The opportunity came as a kind of experiment. The publishers of *The Washington Post* wondered if rush-hour riders on the "Metro"—the city's subway system—would stop their hurried commute long enough to listen to a little violin music. Okay, not a "little" violin music. How about someone like virtuoso Joshua Bell playing something like a 3-million dollar Stradivarius. Okay, not *like* that. *Exactly* that.

As Gene Weingarten, the author of the *Post* article, phrased it, "His performance was arranged by *The Washington Post* as an experiment in context, perception and priorities—as well as an unblinking assessment of public taste: In a banal setting at an inconvenient time, would beauty transcend?"

Who says, "would beauty transcend"? I guess that's why I don't write for *The Washington Post* and Mr. Weingarten does.

So, would people stop and listen? *The Post* asked Leonard Slatkin, music director of the National Symphony Orchestra, his opinion:

> *"Let's assume," Slatkin said, "that he is not recognized and just taken for granted as a street musician. Still, I don't think that if he's really good, he's going to go unnoticed. . . . Out of 1,000 people, my guess is there might be 35 or 40 who will recognize the quality for what it is. Maybe 75 to 100 will stop and spend some time listening."*

> *So, a crowd would gather?*

> *"Oh, yes."*

> *And how much will he make?*

> *"About $150."*

How close was his prediction?

In the 45 minutes that Bell played, seven people stopped what they were doing to hang around and take in the performance for at least a minute. Twenty-seven gave money for a total of just over $32. Another 1,070 hurried by.

Bell said, "It was a strange feeling, that people were actually, ah . . . ignoring me."

Some suggested that the test was flawed, insisting that if people had known it was Joshua Bell playing they would have stopped. People assumed he was just another street musician. Who would risk being late for work to give him their undivided attention?

Yet the part of the story that really got to me was when he described the children who passed by. Weingarten said, "Every single time a child walked past, he or she tried to stop and watch. And every single time, a parent scooted the kid away."

As I read the article, my mind immediately raced to a spiritual parallel. How many people in our busy world encounter Jesus and don't realize who it is they are passing by? People "ignore" Jesus, just as the busy commuters ignored Joshua Bell.

I also felt conviction, thinking, *Maybe people need me to tell them who Jesus is. Maybe all they need is for someone to get their attention and say, "Look! It's Jesus! He's the Son of God. Don't miss this!"*

How sad that people missed the chance to hear a violin virtuoso playing right in front of them. Sadder, still, that people go about their lives without knowing Jesus is right there—right there— wherever they are. They need only stop long enough to hear Him.

As of this writing, The *Washington Post* article appears here: http://www.washingtonpost.com/wp-dyn/content/article/2007/04/04/AR2007040401721.html

The video of Joshua Bell playing in the Metro is on YouTube under the title "Stop and Hear the Music."

Silence

I sometimes read the classic devotional *My Utmost for His Highest* by Oswald Chambers as part of my time with the Lord. I have been known to stumble over the old English and go back and re-read a few lines. Recently, though, I stumbled over the content of the message, not the way it was worded. I read—

"Has God trusted you with a silence—."

Say what? Did that say "trusted you with a silence?" I read it again.

"Has God trusted you with a silence—a silence that is big with meaning?"

Okay, he did say "trusted you with a silence." And then he said silence can be "big with meaning."

This was amazing stuff. I read on.

"God's silences are His answers."

Oh really? If my kids are silent when I ask them a question, I don't accept that as an answer. What does Chambers mean?

"Think of those days of absolute silence in the home at Bethany!"

Now I had to go to the Scriptures to see what Chambers was talking about.

The reference listed was John 11. It's the story of Lazarus. Lazarus' sisters had sent word to Jesus that His dear friend Lazarus was deathly ill. Instead of rushing to the scene, Jesus stayed where He was two more days.

As we know now, Jesus waited those two days so that Lazarus would die and then Jesus could perform the miracle of bringing him back to life. Jesus said, "This sickness is not unto death, but for the glory of God . . . ." After Jesus brought Lazarus back to life, many Jews believed He was the Messiah.

The "silence in Bethany" to which Chambers referred was the two days of waiting the sisters endured after they had sent word to Jesus. Chambers went on to say, "Is there anything analogous to those days in your life? . . . His silence is the sign that He is bringing you into a marvelous understanding of Himself. . . . If God has given you a silence, praise Him, He is bringing you into the great run of His purposes. The manifestation of the answer in time is a matter of God's sovereignty. Time is nothing to God . . . . If Jesus Christ is bringing you into the understanding that prayer is for the glorifying of His Father, He will give you the first sign of His intimacy—silence."

I'm not certain I grasp all of what ol' Oswald is saying, but it does challenge me to be more welcoming of God's silence. When I want a "yes" or "no," perhaps I'll be a bit more patient, realizing that silence is God giving things time to work out for His glory.

Fit Enough

We're not big campers at our house, but we do venture into the woods a few times a year. Most important is our annual trip to Turquoise Lake, a lovely spot near Leadville, Colorado. We've been meeting the same friends there for years. It's the highlight of our summer. Consequently, I'm always on the lookout for new ideas—recipes, activities, packing tips. Once I checked out a book from the library entitled, *Babes in the Woods: The Woman's Guide to Eating Well, Sleeping Well, and Having Fun in the Backcountry*. Sounded perfect.

As it turns out, the author prefers more rustic camping than do I. She likes to hike into remote areas carrying all her gear on her back. The most remote trip I take while camping is from the door of the van to the flap of the tent. I knew early on this woman and I were in different camps, so to speak.

This was never more clear than when I came to a section in her book called, "How Fit Are You? A Simple Test." Allow me to share this exam with you.

First were a couple strength tests.

1. Keeping your back straight (use your legs muscles), lift 35 pounds from the ground to waist height three times.
I skipped this one because I constantly carry 35 pounds at waist level.

2. Walk up and down a flight of stairs (at least twelve steps) carrying 35 pounds of weight three times each.
Too much math here. Twelve, plus 35, times three—next!

Then came the agility tests.

3. Run up and down a flight of stairs—
I was already in trouble on this one—

sideways—
Really?

(your back leg crossing every other step) five times on each side.
I don't think so.

4. Get into a straight-backed chair—
Now this is more my speed.

(the back should be approximately 20 inches high) by climbing over the back of it five times without stepping on any rungs.
She wants me to climb over the back of the chair? Who is going to hold the chair while I do this?

Now for the endurance tests.

5. Sit-ups. (Lie on your back, knees bent, hands at your temples—
Stop there and I'm fine.

—and lift your shoulders completely off the floor) do 15.
Would it count if I lifted one shoulder at a time? I'd do 30 of them. That would equal 15 of her sit-ups.

6. Push-ups. (knees down); do 15.
No.

Okay, so I failed the test, badly. But I don't really need this kind of fitness for my camping trips. My fitness test would be much more practical.

Strength: Carry a lawn chair 20 feet and set it up by a friend's fire.

Agility: Juggle multiple children, tossing red-haired boys between yourself and the mothers of the other red-haired boys.

Endurance: Hike, leisurely, along the lake front until you feel like turning around and going back. Take two or three friends along, and a dog.

That test I pass with flying colors.

With apologies to Bobbi Hoadley, author of *Babes in the Woods*, published by The Globe Pequot Press, Guilford, Connecticut, 2003.

Let's Go Fly a Kite

The Oregon beach is a beautiful thing. Rugged, wild, open. One spring, my four sisters and I spent a week there admiring the ocean's majesty from a beautiful beach house near the small town of Yachats.

The weather was fairly typical Oregon conditions—rainy, cool. But there was enough sunshine for us to walk the beach now and then. We also realized it would be the perfect conditions for kite flying. We stopped in a local souvenir shop and splurged on a few $3.00 kites.

Nancy stepped on the beach, turned her kite to the wind, and the thing took off until her entire length of string was gone. Ellen's kite soon followed. But mine, my kite had some kind of defect. I called it the Kamikaze Kite. It would go up for a second and then turn itself into the sand. It did get up fairly high eventually, but it didn't follow my sisters' kites. It seemed to catch a different current and head off in the opposite direction. Another time, Linda tried to give it a lift, and she nearly lost her head. Bad, kite, bad.

When we came out a couple days later, Nancy loaned me her kite, and I had the same success she did (just in case anyone would want to suggest the problem was operator error).

Jenny and I tried the kites another time, but the wind was just too strong. The kites took off quickly but started twisting and flapping madly. We pulled up our hoods, rolled up the string, and headed inside.

Funny, isn't it, that a kite needs just the right amount of wind in order to soar. Too little wind and nothing happens. Too much wind and it crashes. Kind of like life. If we go along and meet no resistance, no trouble, then we never "get off the ground" as people. It's the difficulties of life that make us better and stronger, more caring and compassionate. Our character is shaped by hardship.

On the other hand, having too many difficulties can send us into a tailspin. We might try to soar, to turn our wings to the wind and fly, but sometimes the trouble is too much for us. That's when we need to roll up the string, pull up our hoods, and head for the protection and safety of home and those we love.

And, like my Kamikaze Kite, if we're not fit to fly, it doesn't matter what the conditions are. Bitterness, pride, greed—various forms of self-centeredness—can keep us from making the most of difficult situations.

I don't know if my sisters and I will ever get back to the beach together, but we have some great photos and wonderful memories. And the $3.00 kites? We left them behind for someone else to enjoy.

Plan B

I love movies. And something I enjoy almost as much as movies are the "behind the scenes" stories *about* movies.

One evening, while flipping through the TV channels, I came upon an interview with movie maker Stephen Spielberg. it was a program called *Spielberg on Spielberg*. He was casually recounting how he got started in the movie business, how he became a director, and what he remembered about some of the movies he's made. And he's made some great movies. *Jaws. Close Encounters of the Third Kind. E.T.—The Extra-Terrestrial. The Indiana Jones* movies. And he's made some unforgettable dramas, like *Schindler's List,* the story of a businessman who rescued Jews in Poland during World War II. It's a movie I watched once and bawled through. I'm not sure I'll ever be able to watch it again.

In this program, Spielberg recalled his early successes. His first three theatrical movies were huge hits—*Sugarland Express, Jaws,* and *Close Encounters*. But then came a lesser-known film called *1941*. Lesser-known because it was less of a film. He admits that he was feeling invincible. And the movie's failure humbled him and taught him to work harder.

But my favorite story came from his recollection about making *Jaws*, a movie based on a novel by Peter Benchley about a gargantuan shark menacing the inhabitants of a quiet, New England village. As production began, a group of designers were still trying to create a mechanical shark to play the part of, well, the shark. In a demonstration, it bubbled its way to the ocean floor.

So Spielberg had to think of another way to make his movie. He couldn't shoot the movie as originally planned, with scenes of the shark attacking people and destroying boats. But he realized he could show the effects of the shark attacks. Anyone who has seen the movie remembers the opening scene of a young woman swimming alone in the water. All of a sudden, she is jerked under water. She goes into a panic, screaming—and then we realize she has been attacked by a shark. But we never see the shark. Speilberg continued to use this approach throughout the movie. We see things being dragged through the water, but it isn't until well into the movie that we actually see the beast.

Spielberg admits that not having the shark until later in production made the movie better. It wouldn't have had the same suspense had we seen the shark all along.

I was inspired by this story to learn to see obstacles as opportunities. Rather than give in when something doesn't work out the way I'd hoped, I need to ask myself, "How else can I do it?"

It's been said, and I agree, that God doesn't have a Plan B. His ways are perfect from the beginning. But from our human perspective, we need be open to a change of plans, a different way, a new approach. I need to view obstacles not as roadblocks but as detours that send me in a new direction. A direction that might even be better than the original route.

Forecast: Snow

The buzz started on Friday. Randy, one of the guys at work, said, "There is a big storm coming for the weekend." Sure enough, meteorologists were sending out the warning. Significant springtime snow storm coming on Sunday.

Saturday, with temperatures in the 50s, saw our neighbors raking the dead grass from the lawn, the folks across the street planting seed. Doug rototilled part of the front yard because we're replanting grass. If it was going to snow on Sunday, we had to get the yard work done Saturday.

I went to the gas station to fill Doug's two-gallon plastic fuel container and noticed a line of cars. It certainly wasn't to take advantage of the prices; it was because snow was forecasted and nobody wanted to run out of gas. I filled the car while I was there.

Later, Kate and I stopped at the grocery store and that, too, had lines of people checking out. Wouldn't want to run out of food during a blizzard. Saw one of my neighbors. She was buying food for her parents so they would be well-supplied. I bought beans for making "One Pot Dinner," a wonderful snow day meal.

The snow was supposed to start falling on Saturday night, but as we went to bed the skies were still clear. Doug woke up early Sunday (as is his practice) and still no snow. By 5:45, though, the white began to fall.

By 8:00 a good three inches blanketed the neighborhood. Church was canceled. (School was canceled the next day.) But we were ready. We got the beans in the crock pot, watched Moody Science Films for "church," made biscuits to go with the beans, and played table games.

All day Saturday I thought, *What if the snow never comes?* Weather predictors have been known to make mistakes. Wouldn't that be funny to have made all these preparations for nothing?

I also had another thought. Jesus' coming is more sure than a snow storm. The predictions in the Bible have never failed. But most people aren't prepared. Maybe they haven't heard the news.

We'd better get the buzz started.

Phone-a-phobia

I suffer from a rather severe case of phone-a-phobia. Phone fear. Okay, fear is a little strong. I'm not actually afraid of the phone or of talking on the phone, I just don't like it very much.

I'm sure it's related to my insecurities and how easily I can be made to feel, well, stupid. When I'm on the phone I feel intense pressure to actually talk. Out loud. And believe it or not, I don't consider myself a "conversationalist." I'm not very good at just chatting.

I remember in the late '70s my dad would drive me from our home in west Boise to the campus of Boise State University (where I attended classes for a whole semester). This took about 20 minutes. Quite often, our conversation would consist of:

"Thanks, have a good day."

"You, too."

Dad wasn't a big talker, either.

The other day I had an experience that only deepened my phobia. I was calling several viola teachers trying to find someone to give Kate lessons. I was calling people I didn't know from a list I'd been given by Kate's orchestra teacher at school.

I called one teacher named "Amy." Now, since I have a niece named Amy who is in her mid-20s, I naturally assumed that this Amy would be of similar age. Why I made such an assumption is unclear, but that was my mindset as I went into the conversation.

After I'd dialed the number I heard a male voice say, "Hello?"

"May I speak to Amy?" I asked.

Silence. Grand pause. Extreme awkwardness and discomfort.

I asked, "Do I have the wrong number?"

"No . . . Why are you calling?"

Perspiration popping on forehead. Heart rate increasing.

"I'm looking for a viola teacher and I'd been given Amy's name."

"Well, we buried Amy about a year ago."

OH NO! I screamed inwardly.

Mind racing. Face getting hot.

This poor man. Probably the young woman's father, still grieving over his daughter's death and here I go calling him out of the blue asking to speak to her.

"I'm so sorry," I finally managed to say out loud.

"Oh, it's okay. She got married and moved to Denver. She doesn't teach down here anymore."

Oh—he had said *married* and I had heard *buried!* Whew, what a relief. "Uh, sorry to bother you," I stammered.

I hung up the phone, heart still racing, face in a serious state of redness. I was embarrassed even though the guy had no idea who I was.

I hate phones! I thought to myself.

I wouldn't really want to be without them, I suppose. Emergencies happen. We do call in a pizza order now and then. But if I never talked on the phone again it would be fine with me.

Later that day I got a call from a dear friend.

"Bec, would you pray for me?"

That's a call I would have hated to miss. Maybe I don't really hate phones after all.

'Tis a Puzzlement

It seemed like a fun idea at the time. Abby and I stood in a checkout line at the local hobby store and there by the register was a table full of puzzles. Not just your average puzzle, mind you. These were "Visual Echo" puzzles that claimed to "dazzle your eyes!" It had a plastic finish on it that made it look 3D. We picked up one with an ocean scene and it looked like some fish were up close and others were way in the back.

"Cool," Abby said.

The puzzle was just a few dollars on an after-Christmas sale. So I bought it.

I took it home and opened it up. It did, indeed, dazzle. With the ribbed plastic coating on every piece it made it difficult to make out the picture underneath. This was going to be a challenge.

And it was. It wasn't a difficult puzzle as puzzles go, it's just that the coating forced me to constantly change the position of the light or lean over the table at odd angles to see the pieces clearly. But as I sat there, bobbing around in my chair, I had time to think, listen to music, and relax. Which is why I enjoy puzzles.

As I sat working on this visual extravaganza, I started making a mental list of things that were true about both puzzles and life. Here are some ideas:

- It's easier when there is a picture to guide you.
- It's best to start with the framework, or "edge."
- Sometimes you have to get up and move to the other side of the table to find the piece you need. A fresh perspective makes all the difference.
- You can sit for long periods making little progress and then— all of a sudden—several pieces fall into place at once.
- You can push and push, but if it ain't right, it ain't right.
- It's more fun with friends and good music.
- Sometimes you just have to give up looking for a piece and move on to something else. Then you'll probably find the piece you were looking for without even trying.
- You have to try a few wrong pieces before finding the right piece.
- Unless a few pieces come out of the box already assembled, the pieces are put together one at a time.

Unlike life, a puzzle has just enough pieces to make things come out perfectly. Things don't always seem to fit together in life. Life is more complicated than cardboard puzzles. Even Visual-Echo-3D-dazzle-your-eyes puzzles. But thankfully we don't have to make all the pieces fit or arrive at some perfect picture when we're done. God is in charge. He sees the big picture, and He'll make things fit into place in a way that's right.

Grace, Grace

Kristen, one of my friends from church, lost her hearing as a child. Though she reads lips amazingly well, at times someone will translate the service into sign language. Usually Kristen's husband, David, does the honors. Some folks purposely sit near Kristen because they're trying to learn sign language. Our family usually sits in that general area, and I find myself being drawn into the beauty of the language.

"Jesus" (a finger tapped on the center of the palm of one hand, then the other, indicating nail prints). "Lord" is the letter "L" (index finger raised, thumb pointing out in the shape of an "L"), drawn from the shoulder to the opposite hip, like the ribbon worn by a beauty contestant. I'm sure the comparison is something else, like royalty, but I always think beauty queen.

"I love you" is expressed with one hand, index finger and thumb making an "L" and the pinky raised making a "y."

I've learned the word for "power." David draws an arc from his shoulder to his elbow—like a Popeye muscle. "Heart" is simply the shape of a heart drawn in the right spot on the chest. But my favorite word is one I learned when Kristen was signing the song

"Marvelous Grace of Our Loving Lord." The chorus is "Grace, grace, God's grace." When she sang the word "grace" she raised her hand just above her face with her fingers straight, tips touching, pointing at her face, like an unopened flower. Then, when she said grace, her fingers burst apart.

I hope I adequately described the motion for you so you can get the same picture I did. It was as if God was showering His grace on her. He does this for all of us, of course. He reaches down and opens His generous hand toward us all.

> *Marvelous grace of our loving Lord.*
> *Grace that exceeds our sin and our guilt.*
> *Yonder on Calvary's mount out-poured,*
> *There where the blood of the Lamb was spilt.*
>
> *Grace, grace, God's grace.*
> *Grace that will pardon and cleanse within.*
> *Grace, grace, God's grace.*
> *Grace that is greater than all our sin.*

Marvelous Grace of Our Loving Lord, Julia H. Johnston and Daniel B. Towner, Hope Publishing, 1910.

Lasting

To celebrate our 25th wedding anniversary, Doug and I went to Breckenridge, a small ski/resort town about two hours from home. For us, the emphasis is on "resort." I've never even tried downhill skiing. I've gone cross country skiing a few times. The best part was singing "Wipe Out" whenever someone in our group fell down. But I digress.

We went in February, even though our anniversary is in July. We went to Breckenridge because we got a call from one of those timeshare people offering us free lodging if we'd attend their 90-minute presentation. We took them up on it figuring we could say no for 90 minutes if it would get us a weekend in Breckenridge. (I have to admit, I felt a little guilty when the time came for the presentation. The saleswoman was very nice and she could have been giving her pitch to someone who had at least a slight interest in buying her product. But, again, I digress.)

One of the reasons we selected this particular weekend was that it was the weekend of the annual snow sculpture festival. Most of the sculptures were still in process when we arrived Friday night. Their deadline was Saturday at 10:00 a.m. And they had to work in the cold. I guess that's to be expected, snow, cold, it's kind of a combo.

The festival is different from other such competitions. The blocks are snow, not ice, trucked off the nearby mountain and dumped into wooden frames, 10 x 10 x 12 feet. The snow is packed by foot, with locals doing the stomping. The process is repeated until there is a solid block.

Sculptors who want to participate In the contest submit a drawing of their idea to the judges several months in advance. The judges select a dozen or so to come compete.

The snow is carved by hand; no power tools. There were sculptures of giraffes, dancers, arches, and more abstract designs. Doug really liked one called "Jazz" that was a sweeping, flowing artsy thing. I liked the elephants, although when they were all finished, I had to admit the jazzy one was pretty cool.

Saturday morning we walked by to see the finished pieces. Then we found a French bakery and had some breakfast. As we ate our croissants, Doug told me about some friends of his who were separated after 10 years of marriage. It felt strange, hearing this news as we were celebrating our 25th.

Sunday morning before heading home we made one more stroll through the sculptures to see if our favorites had won any awards. "Jazz" received second place. My elephants didn't win. First place went to "Old Man Winter," which was a carving of a man's head resting on his fist.

One of the sculptures had fallen overnight. And, of course, they'll all disappear in time. Some things aren't made to last. But, by the grace of God, I think our marriage will stand the test of time.

Elementary, My Dear

Abby has long enjoyed reading Sherlock Holmes mysteries. She said it makes her feel smart. "The mysteries aren't so obvious that you figure it out right away, but they're not so hard that the ending is a complete surprise," she said.

Every once in a while she reads me a good section or tells me of some interesting plot twist. One day, though, what she read was really surprising.

In a story *from The Adventures of Sherlock Holmes* called "The Naval Treaty," we find the great detective standing by a window contemplating a rose.

"There is nothing in which deduction is so necessary as in religion," said he, leaning with his back against the shutters. "It can be built up as an exact science by the reasoner. Our highest assurance of the goodness of Providence seems to me to rest in the flowers. All other things, our powers, our desires, our food, are really necessary for our existence in the first instance. But this rose is an extra. Its smell and its colour are an embellishment of life, not a condition of it. It is only goodness which gives extras, and so I say again that we have much to hope from the flowers."

I've heard people argue that creation declares the existence of God because of its order and design—and I think that's true. But I like Holmes' (actually author Arthur Conan Doyle's) idea, too. Nature, especially the "embellishments," testify of a creative, caring God. He didn't just give us enough. He gave us extra.

True Confessions

I've got a problem. It's time I admit it, get it out in the open and deal with it. My problem: purse passion.

I blame my mother. I have a mental picture of her rapidly changing purses before church on a Sunday morning so her purse would better match her shoes. This taught me that the well-dressed woman matches her purse to her shoes. The less obvious lesson was that a woman is allowed to have multiple purses.

Like most women in my generation, I don't pay a lot of attention to the matching thing, but I've done really well with the multiple purse thing. And they've become progressively larger.

About the time I had children, I resigned myself to the fact that I was a big purse person. I wanted to carry the basic things—wallet, sunglasses, keys—but I also wanted a few extras. I liked my calendar/address book. Pens, lotion. A packet of extra "credit" cards (they weren't credit cards, just that size. Like my children's library cards.) At some point I started carrying what I called my "medicine bag." It's a small, zippered pouch that holds nail clippers, aspirin, a mirror, eye drops. You never know when you might need one of those things. I was definitely a big purse person. I liked the appearance of a small purse and admired women who traveled lightly. But I came to accept my big purseness.

Then, in recent years, my children began to "comment" on the size of my purse. And the weight. I had to admit things were getting a bit out of control.

So, I went in search of the Perfect Purse. I thought it should be a simple design, a neutral color, and about a size 7. You know, like shoes. A nice average size. And it had to have a zipper. My purse has spilled in the car more than once. And for a big purse person that's a big deal.

I found the Perfect Purse at a nearby Ross store. It's a medium brown, a shoulder bag, and about a 6 ½ or 7. But in order to use the Perfect Purse, I had to make some adjustments. I had to give up my lotion bottle. The extra "credit" cards and a few other miscellaneous items. I was quite happy for a while, but then it seemed everything was packed in so tightly, and if everything wasn't in "just so" I couldn't even zip it. I decided I was still a big purse person trying to fit into a small purse. So I went back to a big purse.

But, after a week, I tired of hauling it around. I've decided to see how little I can carry with me everywhere I go. I'm down to a wallet, sun glasses, reading glasses (okay, I'm old), my calendar, a pound of pens and pencils, lip gloss, and mints.

Besides. If I start carrying smaller purses it will give me a reason to buy new ones. Don't I need a small purse for each pair of shoes?

I guess I've still got a problem. But now it's just a smaller problem.

Purses, Foiled Again

I tried. I really tried. I wanted to be a small purse person, even a medium purse person. But it just didn't fit. I'm a big purse person, and I have to accept it.

I've already admitted I have a purse addiction problem. I love purses. But I also admitted I would like to be a smaller purse person. And by that I mean smaller purses, not a smaller person. Although I could make improvement in that area, as well. But I digress. Small purses are cute, and I wanted to be a cute purse person. And by that I mean cute purses, not—well, you know.

But, as I tried to live in a smaller purse, I realized I wasn't happy. I didn't have my nail clippers and my mirror. I didn't have room to tuck in a paperback on the way to the doctor's office. And everyone knows if you don't have a book with you, you end up having to wait twice as long as you would if you had a book with you. So I'm back to carrying big purses with room for a sandwich, a book, and my children's medical records.

After I admitted my purse problem, friends and family began telling me their own purse stories, as if we were part of Purses Anonymous.

Linda carries a small zippered affair with some credit cards and her PDA (Personal Digital Assistant). That and her cell phone is all she carries.

BJ showed me her tiny satchel, and the teeny bottle of lotion she carries in her pocket. My problem is, I don't always have a pocket. Me and Peter Pan.

But I also heard from fellow big purse people. Cindy regaled me with a hilarious account of dumping the entire contents of her big purse on the floor of the card store because she couldn't find her cell phone—which was ringing at the time.

Kim emailed, "I have long admired light-traveling women with cute little purses, but have never had the willpower to join their ranks. The main roadblock is that I've put on all my makeup while driving to work for so many years that I've rendered myself incapable of applying makeup in a stationary building. Therefore my purse must contain my entire makeup kit, in addition to the fingernail clippers, tweezers, hand lotion, sunglasses, pepper spray, cell phone, wallet, keys, coupons, business card holder, vitamin supply, hairbrush . . . ."

Leura wrote a great story, too, but now I can't find it. It's probably in my purse.

Memories of Columbine

Our world is messed up. I'm sure you see evidence of that every day. One of the most disturbing proofs of our fallen world was the shooting at Columbine High School in 1999.

Subsequent shootings—at Virginia Tech in 2007, at a movie theater in Aurora, Colorado, in 2012—always bring Columbine to mind. In the days after the Virginia Tech shooting, everyone had an opinion about why such a thing would happen. People blamed gun control laws, the lack of gun control laws, lax campus security, immigration, and more. Radio personality Rush Limbaugh blamed "the liberals." A few lines from his April 17, 2007 show:

"Well, I'll tell you what, maybe the liberals and their culture of death is the problem, folks. There is a culture of death with liberalism, from abortion on. Embryonic stem cells, euthanasia, you name it. They own that as well as they own defeat in Iraq. Maybe the instant effort to ban God and faith from the public square is a problem here."

I don't think we can blame the liberals. Sorry Rush.

Another opinion attributed to Limbaugh was that the gunman's actions reflect a "cheapening" of human life. People have become disposable because they are disconnected from the "divineness" of their existence, as well as that of others.

That opinion I agree with.

After the Columbine shooting, I wrote a letter to the editor that was published in our local newspaper.

I felt I had to say something to my children about what happened in Littleton. It was sure to come up at school. I told them that a bad man with a gun went to a school in Denver and killed some teenagers.

My second-grade daughter asked, "Mommy, what if the shooters come down here?"

I told her the boys with the guns shot themselves. What a grisly way to calm her fears.

But there is more my children need to know.

They need to know we cannot live in fear, or the bad guys will have won.

They need to know that in times of crisis we need to help each other.

They need to know that while I cannot always protect their physical bodies, their spirits are eternal and cannot be destroyed.

They need to know not to make fun of people who dress or act differently.

They need to know—every day before they go to school—that their parents love them and are waiting for them to come home.

It's a "Get To"

As I left work one day, I mentally reviewed the evening's schedule. *Oh yeah,* I thought. *I have to prepare for Bible study.*

I stopped myself short. *No!* I corrected myself. *I **get** to prepare for Bible study.* I envisioned myself sitting at the dining room table studying the Scriptures, and I realized it was something I enjoy.

The following Sunday night at church, we had a guest speaker recount his experiences teaching Bible classes in a "restricted access" country. He flew into this country at night and met his contact in a coffee shop outside the airport. They identified each other with the false names they'd been told to use.

This man drove the teacher several miles away and dropped him off at the entrance of a dark alley. "Go down that street until someone opens a door and greets you," the man told the teacher. He found his destination and met his class. A group of a dozen or so people had gathered secretly to attend classes for a week. The windows were covered to conceal their activity. They shared a single bathroom and cramped sleeping quarters. But they were happy to be together, delighted to be learning how to study the Bible.

One evening the teacher was asked to lead the class in a Bible lesson—not one of the structured college level classes, but just a lesson for them as a group of believers.

"What shall I teach on?" the teacher asked.

"Our life is hard here," one student told him. "Teach us something that will encourage us."

I wondered what someone could say to encourage a group like this. A group who had family members in prison for following Jesus. Our guest speaker taught them from the book of Isaiah, chapter 26: "The steadfast of mind Thou wilt keep in perfect peace, because he trusts in Thee."

I wondered what I would have taught, and decided I would have said the same things to this group of believers that I say to any of my friends here in America who are discouraged.

I would read Hebrews 13:5,6: "He Himself has said, 'I will never desert you, nor will I ever forsake you.' So that we confidently say, 'The Lord is my help; I will not be afraid. What shall man do to me?' "

I'd share Psalm 55:22: "Cast your burdens upon the Lord, and He will sustain you; He will never allow the righteous to be shaken."

And 2 Corinthians 12:9: "My grace is sufficient for you, for power is perfected in weakness."

Now, when I sit down to study the Bible, I picture my "restricted" brothers and sisters sitting quietly in a darkened room studying the same precious book that I study openly at my dining room table.

Yes, I get to.

Mow De Lawn

When Eric was 11 years old, he celebrated something of a rite of passage. He mowed the lawn.

We were all working outside (pulling weeds mostly) when Doug decided to give Eric his first mowing lesson.

It struck me that Doug never taught his two daughters to mow the grass. I mowed the grass a lot growing up. But then again, with five daughters, my dad couldn't afford to exclude girls from the task. I enjoyed mowing the grass, partly because it was something Dad and I did together. We'd take turns. He'd go a spell, then I'd go a spell. It was a large yard.

Watching Doug and Eric I realized a person really does have to be taught how to do it. It's so intuitive after all these years I can't remember not knowing how. But a person has to learn how to start the mower, how to overlap your rows, and how to complete "the turn." Turning the machine involves pressing down on the handle, not lifting it, as was Eric's first inclination.

He did a good job, and he said he enjoyed it. There were a couple of spots where his rows didn't quite overlap so he cut the long hairs with hand clippers.

All I could think as he worked was, "My little boy is growing up."

At one point, when the mower was quiet, our next-door neighbors came out of their house, smiles on their faces.

"We're going to pick up Christopher at the airport" Cristy called out excitedly. Their son was coming home from college.

Funny, I remember when Christopher was just a kid mowing the lawn.

I Remember Bobby

Every year, as we celebrate Martin Luther King, Jr. Day, I get to thinking about the summer of 1968.

I was just nine years old, living with my family in the small, dusty town of Ontario, Oregon. Being Eastern Oregon, it's not the lush, green rain forest so many people associate with the Northwest. There wasn't much going on there, especially in 1968.

You can imagine the excitement when a bone fide candidate for President of the United States paid us a visit. Robert Kennedy came—in the flesh—to lil' ol' Ontario.

I don't remember much about it. I have a vague mental picture of him standing on an outdoor platform of some kind. I even asked my sisters if they remembered him coming, just in case I had made it up. Two of my sisters remember playing in the high school band for his visit, so I guess it really did happen. The band's performance would explain my presence at the event. I can't picture my parents attending a political rally of any kind, let alone one for a Democrat. I was probably there with my mother, who probably drove my musical sisters to the shindig.

Being young, and as of yet unaffiliated with any political party, I was impressed with the handsome young orator, regardless of what he actually said. Somehow I managed to come home with a black and white, 8 x 10-inch glossy of the man. I think it was even signed. I remember pinning it up on the wall between the studs in our unfinished basement. He was so handsome. I think I had a crush on him.

Not long afterwards I received an early morning phone call from my best friend and next door neighbor Debbie.

"Bobby Kennedy has been shot!" she told me with horror. "He's dead."

I couldn't believe it. Bobby Kennedy was dead.

I hurried to my parents' bedroom and woke them up with the news. "Mom, Dad, Bobby Kennedy has been shot. He's dead," I told them, repeating Debbie's words.

"Hmmph," my mother said, and rolled over. I couldn't believe they didn't share my shock. I'm not sure why they responded that way. Maybe they'd heard it all on the news the night before. Maybe they didn't believe me. Maybe they were just tired. Maybe, they didn't really care.

I wish they had reacted more strongly. If nothing else, they should have cared because I cared. It was sad. I'm also saddened by the fact that I have no recollection of Martin Luther King, Jr.'s assassination two months earlier. I suppose if he had come to Ontario, Oregon, I would have mourned him, too. I should have cared because so many other people cared. But I was just a little white girl, in a dusty town in Oregon, and I didn't know any better. But I remember Bobby.

The Face of Jesus

One day, after being at my job for about a year, one of my co-workers, Jamie, made a casual reference to the portrait of Jesus hanging near our workspace. Up to that point I'd never seen a picture of Jesus on our walls.

"You know that large abstract painting at the end of the hall?" Jamie said. "That's actually a portrait of Jesus."

"No way," I said, lacking a truly clever reply.

"It's true," my boss, Dean, said in support. "Once you see Jesus' face in the painting you don't see the abstract anymore."

So the three of us stood several feet away from the painting as they tried to "show" me Jesus in the painting.

"Squint," one suggested.

"Focus on the black areas," said the other.

"It's just the side of his face. He's looking down."

Finally, after a few more seconds, I saw Him. The black areas were His hair, the white, His face. And Dean was right. Once I saw

Jesus' face, I couldn't see it as an abstract painting anymore.

I was reminded of that experience a few days later when I heard an unusual news report. Apparently, some scientists had "proven" that prayer does nothing to help the sick. I heard this story on our local Christian radio station and the announcer invited people to call in with their opinions on this scientific discovery. People called in and told stories of near death experiences, of cancer disappearing, and other divine interventions.

I decided the problem was that scientists were trying to prove something that was not "scientific." Prayer is an intangible power that can't be measured or graphed. It's something we believe by faith. The Bible tells us a lot about prayer, but it never attempts to define it with a bar graph or pie chart. There is one element of prayer—God Himself—that cannot be measured. Isaiah 55:9 says, "For as the heavens are higher than the earth, so are My ways higher than your ways and My thoughts than your thoughts."

Those of us who believe in prayer see its effects everywhere. Like the painting in my office, life can be seen as an abstract, random series of events, or life can be seen as a masterpiece rendered by the hand of God. The eyes of faith see the face of God at every turn.

Mrs. Who?

"Thank you, Mrs. Groshbosh."

The checker at Safeway tried to follow the store policy of calling a customer by name by reading my name on the bottom of the receipt.

He looked at the bottom of my receipt, made a quick interpretation of "Grosenbach," and came up with "Groshbosh."

I admit, "Grosenbach" is not "Smith" or "Jones" or "Green" or "White" or any of those names a person can decipher at a glance. But it's not rocket science. And it's not Groshbosh.

Most often, if our name is mispronounced it's as GrosenBACK, like your spine, rather than BACH, like the composer. And if it's a passing greeting, like at the grocery store, I just let it go. Actually, mispronunciation is less of an issue than misspelling. For a while I kept a list of how our name was misspelled. We've seen Grossenbach, Grosenback, Goosebeck, Grosenbacker, and many more that I can't recall.

The funny thing is, just about any name is subject to mistake. My maiden name, Odell, was usually pronounced properly but the unfamiliar would inevitably Irish it up a bit and spell it O'Dell. Understandable, I guess, but wrong!

I'm sure whatever your name is you can tell stories of how it has been slaughtered. First names, too. Part of the problem is the English language. We have so many sounds that can be spelled so many ways. In fact, as we decided how to spell our son's name, we considered "Erik," but then we feared people would be tempted to put a "k" on the end of Grosenbach. So then we thought about "Erich," but then we thought people would say "Air-Rich" or something. We went with Eric. That's the way it's spelled by the man he's named after. Sometimes simplicity is the best policy.

I remember at a Grosenbach gathering years ago, we got to talking about our name and Doug's Aunt Ruth said to me, "You know, Becky, we're Grosenbachs by choice," meaning we married into the name, we weren't born with it. And it's a choice I was happy to make. Sure, it's kinda hard to spell and difficult to pronounce, but I'm happy to be a Grosenbach.

I'm just glad Doug's last name isn't Schwarzenegger. Although the Safeway checker probably would have gotten that one right.

The $23 Prom Dress

Abby attended her first prom her sophomore year of high school. She went with Tony, a senior who lived down the street from us. Nice boy. Just friends.

A few weeks before the prom, we started shopping for a dress.

"Prom dresses can cost $100," I said one night over dinner, wanting to warn Doug that this might be a pricey venture. "But we'll see if we can find something for less. We'll go to Ross tonight and if we can't find anything there, we'll make a trip to the mall."

We live less than a mile from a Ross store, so we knew we could fit in a quick trip that night. Before we went into the store, Abby and I prayed in the van. (Which, by the way, we named "Lieutenant Van, Lieutenant Van," which must be said twice in your best Forrest Gump imitation.) We asked the Lord to help us find just the right dress for a "good price."

Amazingly (why I should have been amazed I don't know, we did pray), we found not just one but two dresses she liked. And they were both marked down to $23.00. (We got them both. There would be other dances.)

She went with a white, below the knee dress, sleeveless. Very pretty. And we were so proud of ourselves (and God) that we spent only $23.00.

Unfortunately, she only had casual white sandals at home. That would never do. We went next door to Payless. White dress shoes: $22.00.

The next day Abby said, "Ya know, Mom, that dress isn't as fancy as I had originally hoped, so it would be great if I could have my hair done so that the hairstyle would kind of compensate for the less fancy dress."

"I'll think about it," I told her.

The only other time Abby had had her hair done was for a wedding, and someone else paid for it. Abby thought it cost $60.00. That's a lot of money for a hairdo.

I called around and found a place that would do it for $45.00. But even that seemed like a lot to pay. But I also knew I couldn't fix her hair the way she wanted it.

Somehow, Kate caught wind of the fact that Abby wanted her hair done and I wasn't so sure I wanted to pay $45.00 for it. One morning, as I drove her to school, Kate said, "You only paid $23.00 for the dress, right? What if you had found a dress for $45.00? Would you pay $23.00 for Abby to get her hair done?"

Somehow that made sense. So I made the appointment.

Before we went to the salon, I wanted Abby to have a picture to show the hairdresser, so we went to Safeway and found a magazine full of hairstyles. Abby found a style she liked, so I bought the magazine. $7.00.

Then I realized Abby would need some kind of jacket to wear with the dress. The forecast said, "Cooler, chance of rain." Plus, Abby asked if I had a purse she could borrow (don't get me started on purses). However, even my vast supply of purses didn't yield anything she could use. So we went to Target. Jacket: $27.00. Purse: $22.99.

Even though Tony bought the prom tickets and took Abby out for dinner, I couldn't send her off without any money. $20.00 cash.

So our $23.00 dress mushroomed into $167.98. But when Abby stood in front of the mirror before Tony picked her up she said, "I feel like a princess."

Priceless.

The Piano Recital

One chilly Saturday afternoon when Abby was in high school, Doug, Abby, and I attended a piano recital featuring our friend Claire. We've known Claire and her family for years, through camping, church, even karate class. Abby pointed out in the car on the way there, "This may be one of Claire's last recitals since she'll graduate high school this year."

Of course, that made me extra emotional during Claire's piece. I started to tear up a little, thinking about how quickly Claire, her brother Hollis, and our kids, had grown. Truth is, I cry at everything, so I probably would have cried anyway. But the "last recital" thing was a good excuse.

The recital featured several pianists, all students of the same teacher. Claire was the best, not that I'm biased. Claire is quite accomplished. She even does those things where you run your finger across the length of the keyboard. That's got to hurt. She played a two-piano duet with her teacher. In fact, every song was a duet, and almost every one of them a teacher/student duet.

Since most of the students were beginners, the teacher and student played side by side on the same piano, the teacher playing the lower parts, the student playing higher. Sometimes the student played a one-note-at-a-time melody while the teacher filled in with more complicated harmonies and rhythms.

The teacher adapted her tempo to stay with the student, while still trying to maintain an even speed, sometimes slightly nodding her head to indicate the beat. Nerves got the best of one girl and she fumbled and then stopped playing altogether. The teacher calmly pointed to a spot on the music and they started again.

The duets were masterfully arranged. The less accomplished pianists sounded marvelous with their teacher playing a more difficult accompaniment. Those who were more advanced still benefited from the fuller sound of four hands playing together.

It reminded me of Romans 8:26 and 27: "In the same way, the Spirit helps us in our weakness. We do not know what we ought to pray for, but the Spirit himself intercedes for us with groans that words cannot express . . . The Spirit intercedes for the saints in accordance with God's will."

Like a novice pianist, my prayers are often simple, one-note-at-a-time expressions of what is on my heart. I want to offer eloquent praise or profound intercession. But truth is, I'm just an ordinary person who doesn't really know how to express herself to God. Sometimes I just sit in silence, unable to say a word.

Thankfully, God understands our limitations. He gave us the Holy Spirit, Someone who understands prayer, Someone who knows God's will, Someone who can take my simple words and make them sound right. Someone more accomplished at addressing the Father prays with me. And, through the Holy Spirit, my prayers become music to the Father's ears.

Pacemaker . . . Peacekeeper

God is our refuge and strength, a very present help in trouble.
Therefore we will not fear . . . (Psalm 46:1,2).

These verses took on new meaning for our family back in the fall of 2006.

Over Labor Day weekend, Doug started experiencing some strange symptoms. He felt light headed and dizzy at times. He was tired. And he felt some "tightness" around his heart. Now, anytime someone includes the word "heart" in his list of symptoms, it should be cause for concern. But Doug went about his normal routine, and I just didn't think anything serious was going on. Not my best moment as a wife.

My sister Nancy, who as visiting us at the time, asked Doug when he was going to see the doctor about his symptoms. Doug said, "Oh, he'll just tell me to get more exercise and lose some weight." But when Doug arrived at work on Wednesday, his co-worker, Jerry, said, "You don't look so good. Come with me," and marched Doug to the company's resident nurse.

She took Doug's blood pressure. Fairly normal. She took his pulse: 56. A normal pulse is more like 70. She recommended he see a doctor. Soon.

Doug called our doctor's office and was able to get in at 11:30 that morning. Doug called me before he went to the doctor's office just to let me know what was going on.

I'm glad he did, because it lessened the shock of the next phone call:

"Becky, Dr. V. checked my pulse and it was 48. He did an EKG and during the EKG my pulse dropped to 41. Dr. V. didn't like what he saw in the EKG reading so he faxed it to a cardiologist. The cardiologist said, 'This patient needs a pacemaker.' "

When Doug told me that, my brain heard, "This patient needs to have a series of tests done to determine if he does, in fact, need a pacemaker someday, say 30 years from now." But Doug went on to say, "Dr. V. said I need to have someone come pick me up and take me to the hospital." It started to register that this was something of an emergency.

I left work and met Doug at the doctor's office. On the way to the hospital, Doug finally got me to understand that a surgeon had been contacted and the procedure was to take place later that same day.

He was on his way to the hospital to get a pacemaker.

By this time he'd made a number of phone calls and people were already praying for us. After we arrived at the hospital I continued to call friends and family. I called our neighbor, Cristy, and asked her to keep Eric with her for a couple hours after school. She graciously agreed, and even took on the weighty responsibility of explaining to a 10-year-old boy why his father was in the hospital. (When I got home later that afternoon, Eric understood more about pacemakers than I did.)

Doug eventually got checked into room 3017—after telling the nurses he was checking in because he'd heard the food was good—and began to wait. He was hooked up to several monitors. His pulse: 38.

And wait we did. The surgery we thought was going to happen Wednesday night was rescheduled to 10:00 Thursday morning. Then to 1:00 Thursday afternoon.

I became pretty familiar with Room 3017. There was a framed photograph on the wall. It showed a majestic mountain scene with a sea of purple wildflowers in the foreground. On the matte was a brass plate with this inscription: "God is our refuge and strength, a very present help in trouble. Therefore we will not fear . . ." (Psalm 46:1,2).

How fitting, I thought. *Not just for us, but for anyone who occupies this room.*

We had company. Our friend, Elaine, from church. All three of our pastors at different times. Doug's boss, Tom. Our friend Bob. Bob and Linda have "been there" for us during many crisis situations so I was not surprised to see him. Pleased, but not surprised. Bob brought with him a card their daughter, 14-year-old Mary, had made for Doug. She had written a verse on the front of the card: "God is our refuge and strength, a very present help in trouble" (Psalm 46:1).

Doug finally went into surgery around 2:45 Thursday afternoon. His pulse before surgery: 30. An hour later: 72.

I learned a lot about the heart, about pacemakers, and pacemaker surgery. The pacemaker was installed just below Doug's left collar bone. Two wires run through a vein to his heart and supplement his natural electrical impulses. Everything else about Doug's heart is great—the valves work fine, the various vessels are clear, and the muscles are strong. He just had an electrical problem.

We were all relieved when he came home Friday morning. We so appreciated the concern, prayers, and support of our neighbors, our church, and family and friends across the country. My friend Cathy sent me an e-mail from Atlanta:

"I don't know when you'll get this, but my prayer is that you will read this e-mail when you need it most. This morning my daily Bible reading was Psalm 46. Psalm 46:1 and 2 says, 'God is our refuge and strength, a very present help in trouble. Therefore we will not fear . . . .' "

Yes, we learned a lot about pacemakers that week. But we also learned to lean on our Great Peacekeeper, our ever-present help and strength.

The Cuteness Factor

Have you heard of the cuteness factor? That's when the cuteness of the performer is measured against the actual skill demonstrated in the performance. Small children generally have a high cuteness factor. Execution may score low, but cuteness will score high, raising the overall score of the performance. That's the cuteness factor.

Case in point, the four-ish-year-old boy who played the teeny tiny violin at Kate's recital one year. The recital was for all the students of Kate's private viola teacher (who also teaches some violin students). This little guy played two songs, the first called "From D to E." The title was not some cryptic message about making forward progress in life or anything like that. The song consisted of two notes, and I'm fairly certain the notes were "D" and "E." He played pizzicato, meaning he plucked the strings. At the completion of the song, he paused, kept the violin under his chin and extended his right hand. His teacher placed his bow in his hand, and the mini-maestro set bow to string and played "Twinkle, Twinkle, Little Star."

When he finished, he placed his violin at his side, stuck his chin in the air to gain momentum, and bowed at the waist to abundant applause. Huge cuteness factor with this performance.

Kate was hoping for a few points from the cuteness factor. She wore a new dress and did, indeed, look very cute. She said, "Well, if I mess up, I might as well look good doing it." She didn't mess up. She played "Prelude to Suite #1 in G Major." You'd recognize it if you heard it. It was written for cello but she played it on her viola. Not perfectly, but beautifully. I was proud.

Perfection wasn't the goal. Everyone there made mistakes. But Kate stood alone in front of a room full of people (including her parents, sister, and brother—and her teacher) and played very well. She worked hard and did her best.

The cuteness factor counts when you're four. When you get older, you need to score high on other things—preparation, dedication, and courage. It may not earn you man's applause, but you can still take a bow for a job well done.

Kindle,
Barnes and Noble

If our local Barnes and Noble bookstore were any indication, I'd say print communication was alive and well. It's an enormous store filled with books on travel, science, history—any topic you could imagine.

Yet I know traditional publishing is in trouble. It's expensive to print books these days. And with the invention of electronic books, people can download a book off the Internet for much less than it costs to buy a print version, and they can carry multiple books with them in a device about the size of *Reader's Digest*. Barnes and Noble has a version called a Nook. Amazon released the Kindle.

I recently looked over the shoulder of a friend as he explained his Kindle to a couple of us. He can enlarge the size of the type— a real advantage to those of us who wear reading glasses—and copy portions of the book to be saved in a separate document. My friend is one of those who goes through a few books a week, so his Kindle serves him well. He can get a new book without leaving his chair. No trip to the library or Barnes and Noble.

"I can be sitting in the airport and purchase a new book in less time than it would take someone else to walk across the waiting area to the bookstore and purchase a hard copy," he illustrated.

I'm kind of torn between my love of books and my love of electronic organizing. To think I could copy portions of a book and save them in a document, all referenced, to review later for an article or a speech—that would be pretty sweet. But I'm torn. I love the smell of books, the feel of the pages. And I adore magazines— seeing them displayed on the newsstand, reviewing the headlines in the supermarket, reading in the car as I wait for a child to get out of school, cutting out my favorite recipes to file in my recipe book (or stick in a file box to someday be pasted in a book). And you don't have to worry about a magazine's battery running low or interfering with an airplane's take-off or landing. And if a printed book "crashes," you can just bend over and pick it up.

I think I'm going to have to give up on print, though. I really believe things are going electronic. But as I look around the bookstore at the beautiful leather bound journals and glossy magazine covers it makes me sad . . . .

Lucky Me

I won a drawing today. I attended a luncheon with a group of people I'd never luncheoned with before, and I won a book in a random drawing.

It happens to me all the time. A few months ago I won a painting in a drawing at work. Last fall I won concert tickets by being the ninth caller to a radio show. I won $1,000 once by calling a radio station when they played the song of the day. Which just happened to be "Windy," the song my third grade class sang for a school program.

All the other classes were singing "Edelweiss" from *The Sound of Music* but our class was singing a song by The Association. Our teacher bought the 78 and we played it over and over again on our little classroom record player until we had all the words transcribed. We didn't have the option of finding the lyrics on the Internet.

Yeah, my third grade teacher was cool. I wish I remembered her name. Aiken Elementary School, Ontario, Oregon, 1967. She had a blonde beehive and wore pink lipstick and miniskirts. She's the teacher I credit with igniting my love for writing. Actually, it started with poetry. My teacher liked a poem I'd written for a class assignment, and I was a changed person.

I can remember sitting in my bedroom closet with a flashlight—probably looking for a place to be alone—and writing a dictionary of rhyming words. When somebody as cool as my third grade teacher says you're good at something, it's pretty inspiring.

My sister Jenny tells a story that once when she asked me what I wanted to be when I grew up I said, "I don't know, but I want to write poetry in my spare time."

So anyway, I won a book today. It happens to me all the time.

No Dogs, Just Peeves

My friend Kim sent me an e-mail at work that quoted three lines of a song. (Yes, it was work related. Sorta.) I e-mailed her back with the last line; you can't leave a song unfinished.

That reminded me of the way I used to torture my sister Jenny. I was in high school, the annoying little sister of the house. Jenny was in college, a music major. I would play a song on the piano, poorly, because that is the only way I can play, and when I'd reach the end of the song, I'd leave off the last chord. Or play it wrongly.

Poor Jen just couldn't stand it. She'd come out of whatever far-reaches of the house she was in and hit that last chord. Correctly.

But it's all coming back to haunt me. I've discovered there are things people can use to annoy me, too. You'll notice my use of the adverbs "wrongly" and "correctly." One of my pet peeves is when people don't "ly" their modifiers. Abby turns up the radio when George Strait sings "It Just Comes Natural." Like my sister before me, I'll come from the furthest recesses of the house to add the "ly" every time he sings that line. And the really annoying thing is, he could easily fit the "ly" into the song. Instead of singing, "Nat-ur-al" he could just as easily sing "Natch-ra-ly." Please!

And then I was at Eric's school one day and noticed a pencil dispenser. Good idea, a pencil dispenser. I checked out the machine and the instructions were to insert a quarter and pull out the lever "slow." SLOW. How about "SLOWLY," if you please.

But it got worse. On the front of the machine it says, "Unsharpened pencils with erasures." I read it twice. I asked Kate, who was with me at the time, to spell the word "eraser."

"E-R-A-S-E-R," she said. She passes to the next round.

"Erasure," of course, is the act of erasing, that action that leaves a little smudge on your paper. For example, your math teacher might say, "There are too many erasures on your homework." At least that's why my math teachers used to say.

Maybe the pencil vending machine really meant "erasures." Maybe along with a new pencil it delivered little slips of paper with smudges on them. But I doubt it.

Now, I don't claim to speak perfect English, nor do I speak English perfectly. But I am annoyed by the misuse of "ly." And don't get me started on the use of the apostrophe. I actually tried to erase one once at the local hot dog stand. On the dry erase board they had written "Winner's" and underneath posted the punchcards of people who had won a free hot dog. I'm pretty sure they meant "Winners" because they didn't list any possessions of said winner. So I actually tried to rub off the apostrophe. But it wasn't erasable. Which I'm not sure is a word at all.

So, ya see. We all have our pet peeves, don't we? Mine just come natural. Ly.

Mary Pickersgill's Flag

Pickersgill. It's an unusual name. Unusual, but fitting, for Mary Pickersgill was given an unusual task.

In the midst of The War of 1812 between the British and the Americans, Mary Pickersgill, a widowed Baltimore flag maker, was asked to sew a flag. But not just an ordinary flag. Major George Armistead wanted a big flag, a very big flag, to fly over Fort McHenry at the entrance to Baltimore Harbor. So Mary and her 13-year-old daughter, Caroline, spent weeks in the summer of 1813 assembling a flag measuring 30 feet by 42 feet. That's as big as almost 30 ping pong tables.

By September of 1814, the British had burned Washington, D.C., and were bombing Fort McHenry from land and sea. An American attorney was watching the battle from aboard a British ship, having just negotiated the release of an elderly physician who had been taken captive. The battle continued into the night until the British abandoned the attack, judging it would be too costly to complete the task. As the smoke cleared and the sun rose, this attorney saw Mary Pickersgill's flag flying over Fort McHenry. He was inspired to write these words:

Oh, say can you see,
By the dawn's early light,
What so proudly we hailed at the twilights' last gleaming?
Whose broad stripes and bright stars, through the perilous fight,
O'er the ramparts we watched, were so gallantly streaming?

Yes, Mary Pickersgill's flag became known as the Star Spangled Banner. The flag survives to this day and hangs in the Smithsonian Institution's National Museum of American History. Mary Pickersgill's home has been converted into a museum called Flag House.

Pickersgill. It is an unusual name. But it's a name forever linked with The Star Spangled Banner, an unforgettable flag.

<http://www.flaghouse.org/about/a_hist.html >

Source: *Honor Our Flag*, David Singleton, The Globe Pequot Press, 2002

Lilacs

Abby has declared May 14 to be National Lilac Day. The fact that May 14 is also Abby's birthday is completely coincidental. Okay, entirely intentional.

Abby looks forward to having lilacs on her birthday. But, here in Colorado, we don't always get them. At least in our yard. Sometimes we'll get freezing temperatures just as the blossoms are about to open and all the flowers are lost. And sometimes other conditions just aren't right—not enough, sun, not enough water.

But then there are those springs when the conditions are perfect—oh, my. Our two bushes become heavy with white and purple flowers. All over town bushes burst with color.

But greater than the visual splendor of the lilacs is the fragrance. We can open a window and breathe in sweet perfume. We walk around the block and smell the flowers before we see them.

Many analogies come to mind. Like the fact that a hard winter often precedes a wondrous spring, just like life's difficulties give blossom to a stronger person. And the idea of having "the right conditions" for us to bloom. Without the water of the Word of

God or the refreshment of prayer, how can we expect to thrive?

But the lesson that came to me over and over again was that of being the fragrance of Christ.

"Through us, he brings knowledge of Christ. Everywhere we go, people breathe in the exquisite fragrance. Because of Christ, we give off a sweet scent rising to God. . ." (2 Corinthians 2:14, *The Message*).

How I would love to come into someone's presence and have her think, "She is so pleasant to be around," or "She always has something positive to add to the discussion." And, oh, to have them credit not me but our Savior!

I want to be lilacs. Not just in May, but every day of the year.

The Eagle Has Landed

"One small step for man; one giant leap for mankind."

I clearly recall hearing those words on July 20, 1969, the day man first walked on the moon.

I got to skip Sunday evening church to watch the moon landing. And we never skipped church. I felt a little guilty, but this was the moon landing. I wasn't going to miss it. I remember my mother and one of my sisters went to church and got back home before the astronauts actually walked on the moon. I remember seeing my mother and sister walk past the basement window and thinking how ironic it was that they went to church *and* got to see man walk on the moon. Though I'm sure "ironic" was not in my 10-year-old vocabulary. While I can picture myself in the family room watching the moon landing, it's the skipping church part that remains most vivid in my mind. That says something about my family, I guess. Moon landing, skipping church, equally monumental.

I remember my father telling me that when he was in high school his science teacher told his class that man would walk on the moon in their lifetime. "We all thought he was crazy," Dad said.

Wonder if that teacher was still alive in 1969. I hope so.

Like most Americans during those years I was enamored with space. I had a poster in my bedroom of "The Earth Rising," a now famous image of the "half earth" suspended in a black sky above the surface of the moon. The space program gave us all something to be proud of in a time when our country was greatly divided over a great many things.

Years later I watched a documentary about the moon landing. It brought up some things I didn't realize as a child. Nixon was president. (I knew that.) He spoke to the astronauts by phone by way of the Houston Space Center. (Why don't I remember that?) Five other Apollo missions landed on the moon, the last one in 1972. I knew there were other missions to the moon, but I couldn't have told you there were that many. The Six Flags amusement parks ought to capitalize on that somehow.

The documentary also talked about the importance of Apollo missions 1 through 10. Each one tested an important part of the moon landing, with Apollo 10 hovering above the surface of the moon without actually landing.

As I watched the documentary, I noticed I was smiling. I was reliving the excitement of those space travel years. I smiled realizing I remembered the day man walked on the moon. I shared that experience with "my fellow Americans." And I was proud.

Cindy, It's Your Cell Phone

My friend Jane once observed that cell phones don't ring; they call out to you.

This has never been more true than it is for my friend and co-worker Cindy.

Our department, and indeed most of the building, is divided into cubicles. We tend to hear most of what's going on around us. If I sneeze, half a dozen people offer up, "Bless you."

In that setting we begin to recognize each other's cell phone rings. Kendra has "Who Can It Be Now?" Tim's is the theme from the Harry Potter movies. And then there's Cindy's.

Cindy's 20-something daughter, Jillian, recorded a custom "ring" for Cindy's phone. When Cindy's phone goes off we hear Jillian's voice saying, "Cindy, it's me, your cell phone! I'm ringing! I'm in your purse . . . in the middle pocket . . . next to your keys . . . no, keep digging . . . a little deeper . . . behind your wall—there ya go!"

Every time it starts we all secretly hope it will take Cindy a while to answer so we can hear the whole message.

The first day Cindy arrived at work with this unique ring tone we all had to hear her story.

Cindy was unaware that Jillian had recorded this message to act as the phone's ring tone. Until she was at the doctor's office.

For this particular exam, Cindy had to change her clothes and secure all her belongings in a locker. Returning to the changing room at the end of her appointment she hears a voice: "It's me . . ."

The voice is familiar.

". . . I'm in your purse . . ."

It sounds like Jillian.

". . . in the middle pocket . . ."

Then another woman in the dressing room looks at Cindy in a panic. "I think there's a child locked in there!" the lady says, pointing toward Cindy's locker.

Cindy quickly opened the locker to discover her phone had been "calling" her, quite literally.

Sometimes cell phones can interrupt and annoy. But other times, especially for Cindy, the phone brings the sound of a familiar voice. And a smile.

Things I Miss from Childhood

Here are a few things I miss from my childhood days:

The complete lack of responsibility. My mother even fed the dog. But lack of responsibility also meant a lack of freedom. I was pretty much at the mercy of those with cars and the license to drive.

My dog. Pebbles was a chihuahua mixed with who knows what else. She wasn't a particularly nice dog, at least not to strangers. But she loved our family. I can remember getting her to chase me as I ran around the house. Then I'd turn around and chase her. She could sure run, that little thing.

Roller skating with one skate in the garage. We had one pair of roller skates in our family. They were the kind that you'd clamp on your shoes. My sister Ellen and I would each strap on one skate (I don't remember if I had the same skate every time or not) and skate in circles in the garage. Dad kept it clean and it gave us a large, smooth surface. Push-glide . . . push-glide . . . There was something special about it. Sharing, making do . . . .

Dance routines with Jerilyn. One of my best friends in late grade school was my church friend, Jerilyn. I got to spend the night with her once, and we made up a routine to the song "Seattle" by Bobby Sherman. I've long since forgotten the steps, except that when we'd sing the word "Seattle" we'd stop and extend an arm toward a painting on the wall of her living room—as if the painting were of the soggy city. Dancing was frowned upon at my house, so dancing—to the music of Bobby Sherman, no less—was like enjoying a forbidden pleasure.

The farm. The farm was my maternal grandparents' home in Iowa. The house was a simple two-story building, with a rarely used front porch. Everyone came in through the side door, between the kitchen and the cellar. Grandpa was a quiet, stoic farmer who didn't go out of his way to impress anybody. Granny, on the other hand, fretted over everything and everybody. She made sure there were filled candy dishes in every room, bottles of pop on the cellar steps, and ice cream bars in the freezer. And I loved the farm itself. Fields of corn, noisy crickets, smelly cows.

Riding my bike. I would go for long rides by myself, for what seemed like hours. If my kids did that today, I'd worry about their safety. But there wasn't much to worry about in Boise. Once, I rode with my friend Karen all the way downtown. My friend Becky and I rode to our favorite spots where we'd climb trees or catch snails. My bike was a way to get to special places. But it was also a joy in itself. Just riding, riding, riding. Sometimes I'd rubber band my dad's transistor radio to the handlebars and enjoy some music as I rode along. I guess this doesn't have to be something I miss; I could still ride a bike today. But I rarely do.

What's the common thread? I think it's finding joy in the simple, carefree pleasures of life. Yeah, I miss that. Being a grown-up isn't as much fun. But at least I get to drive the car.

Soup, Salad, and Serious Conversation

I had soup and salad at the Olive Garden with my friend Julie not long ago. After a little chitchat, she said she wanted to ask me a question. She locked her big blue eyes to my brown ones and asked, "How do you not worry about things and have faith?"

I knew Julie's question was not academic. She was worried. Her husband had asked for a divorce. I'd be worried, too.

I reminded Julie of Philippians 4:6. A paraphrase of this verse is, "Don't worry about anything; instead, pray about everything."

I encouraged Julie to pray, but admitted that even so, we're still likely to worry. When I got home I read Philippians 4:6-8. It says,

"Be anxious for nothing, but in everything by prayer and supplication with thanksgiving let your requests be made known to God. And the peace of God, which surpasses all comprehension, shall guard your hearts and your minds in Christ Jesus. Finally, brethren, whatever is true, whatever is honorable, whatever is right, whatever is pure, whatever is lovely, whatever is of good repute, if there is any excellence and if anything worthy of praise, let your mind dwell on these things."

As I read these verses, I realized there was a lot more I should have told Julie. Here's what I should have said:

There are two little words in verse 6 that I tend to forget: with thanksgiving. Even in the midst of divorce and all the pain you're going through, find something to thank God for. There are other things in your life, other people in your life, that you can thank God for. Make a list of you want to, and review it when you start to worry. But even if it's the same thing every day, thank God for that one thing.

Another key is that long list of virtues in verses 7 and 8. Don't let your mind fixate on the negative things that are going on in your life right now. When you find your thoughts drifting back to things that make you angry or sad, remind yourself of something that is true and honorable. Something like, "I will survive this. God will bring something good out of it." Those things are true.

Or think of something you love. Think about your daughter spilling her drink down her arm in class. Look at the mountains. Okay, funny and beautiful aren't on the list. But those are still good things to think about.

This is also where reading your Bible will help. It's full of things that are excellent and lovely. I like to read Psalms when I need to get my mind in the right place.

God says He will give us peace, which is the opposite of worry. We need to pray, be thankful, and think of good things.

And you also need to have lunch with your friends on a regular basis. Meet you at Olive Garden.

Chef Eric

Ever since he was young, my son, Eric, has loved to cook. I remember the night he made sausage gravy for dinner. This excited me on several levels.

1) Eric was a good cook.

As a kid he loved watching the popular and charismatic chef Emeril Lagasse on television. Eric isn't afraid to experiment and try new things. I'm tied to recipes and seldom deviate.

He helped make hamburgers on the grill one night. They needed a little extra cooking time in the microwave, but otherwise turned out really good.

"Did you put something extra in the meat?" someone asked.

"No."

"Did you grill them differently?"

"No, all I did was shape them into patties," he said.

He must have magic hands if he just has to pat the meat for it to turn out just right!

2) Eric was 13.

I didn't know how to make gravy until after I was married. I was amazed that Eric could make gravy—and good gravy—at age 13.

3) Eric was part of our family support network.

When I was offered the option to work full-time after working part-time for a few years, I asked my family what they thought about it. One of my concerns was getting dinner on the table every night. I could join the ranks of those who cook once a week—or once a month—and prepare enough food for a week— or a month. But I'm not that organized. Nor do I want to be. My family offered to share the cooking chores. Each of us (Doug, the three kids, and I) agreed to cook one weeknight and clean up one weeknight. Doug and I would work together on weekends.

We set the schedule around each person's availability. We each had regular activities like music lessons or meetings that we needed to accommodate. Plus, short-term activities, like play practice, required a little flex in the schedule.

I can't say we all did our chores without grumbling, but we did get it done. And we learned to cook and clean and cooperate. Talk about life skills!

4) I love sausage gravy.

'nuf said.

How to Spot
an Out-of-Towner

Living in Colorado, I see wildlife on a regular basis. I've had foxes and raccoons in my yard and big horn sheep outside my office window. Not so for other people.

My friend Cindy's sister, Barb, works at one of the local hotels frequented by business travelers and tourists. One day after work, on her way to her car, Barb saw a man jogging on the path behind the hotel. As she watched him, she realized he wasn't out for some casual exercise; this man was running full out. He looked over his shoulder, panic on his face, then ran straight toward Barb.

As he approached her, Barb reached for her cell phone. He stopped in front of her, panting, hand clutching his chest.

This man is having a coronary, Barb thought. "Shall I call 911?" she asked him.

He shook his head, raising a hand toward her, steeling another glance over his shoulder.

"I should know this—" (pant, pant) "—I've seen it—" (pant, pant)

"—on TV," he finally managed. "Do you—" (pant, pant) "—make eye contact? Am I supposed to raise my arms—" (pant, pant) "—over my head and get real big?"

O dear! Barb thought. *Is he being chased by a mountain lion? A bear?*

He gasped for air again. "What do you do," he asked her, "when you see . . . a deer?"

You Can Trust Your Car

When our children were teenagers, they completed a formal drivers education course taught by Mr. Matthews, a friend of ours in the drivers ed business. The course included the usual book learnin' and four driving sessions where Mr. Matthews took them on residential roads, city streets, and the freeway.

Before teenagers can receive a driver's license in Colorado, they are required to complete a certain number of driving hours under adult supervision in both daytime and nighttime. The state also limits the number of passengers teens can carry for the first several months. If Colorado didn't set these rules, Doug and I would have. I've heard too many stories about cars full of teenagers crashing and . . . . Yes, we'd already decided our children wouldn't drive cars full of friends.

It's quite different from when I learned to drive. I took a week of classes, a few loops around town with my teacher, and I was licensed to drive. My sister Ellen gave me another course in driving my father's Datsun (it was a stick shift), but there were no limits on passengers and such. I soon had my first speeding ticket, issued while I was driving a few of my friends around. I haven't had a speeding ticket since, I might add.

Anyway, because the kids had to have 50 hours each of supervised driving hours, it fell on Doug and me to ride shot gun and advise. Doug did a lot more of this than I did. He'd take them out driving for hours at a time, just so they could get their time in. I may have done that once or twice. I wasn't eager to submit my personal well-being, my family's well-being, and, yes, my vehicle's well-being to a novice driver.

It was a little easier for me when Doug was in the front seat with one of the newbees. I knew he was able to reach over and correct steering or rescue us from a bad lane change.

It reminded me a little of the Christian life. Like a new driver, I may think I'm the one in control. I think I'm the one making all the decisions. But I'm not. God is the trustworthy one. His wisdom guides, His hand directs.

Eventually the kids all became licensed drivers. Now they can drive on their own without Mom or Dad. But even so, they're still under God's watchful eye. I'm learning to trust God in a whole new way.

Conflict Resolution

One Sunday, in the church foyer, our friend Lynn told us, "I'm moving!" Tears welled in her eyes and she explained how her company had been sold and was to be relocated to a place called Mississippi.

"I really am excited about it," Lynn said. "It's going to be hard to leave, but good, too." She was happy and sad at the same time.

I had a similar experience one winter weekend when all three of our children were away from home, leaving Doug and me with a couple of days to ourselves. We watched a video, did some research on the internet, drove to the mountains. At one point I told Doug, "It's been really nice spending time just us two." He agreed.

But at the same time I missed our children. I wondered what they were doing, if they were safe, having fun.

How could I enjoy not having the kids around and miss them at the same time? How could both be true? Seemingly conflicting emotions sharing equal billing.

In a much larger, more profound fashion, our God possesses seemingly conflicting attributes. Somehow He is loving (wishing none would perish) and just (unable to tolerate sin). He is the controller of all things and yet invites our participation with Him through prayer.

The Bible teaches things about God that seem to conflict with each other, but because the Bible says it, I accept both to be true. Faith (which the Bible says is a gift from God) allows me to believe that two seemingly conflicting ideas can both be true at the same time and place.

Sometimes it would be nice if everything about God could be packaged up and tied with a neat little bow. But on the other hand, I'm glad He's bigger than my ability to understand. If I understood everything about Him, He would cease to be God.

"Your" Kidding, Right?

One day, while driving around town doing a bunch of errands, I pulled up next to a minivan with the following message spelled out in three-inch red vinyl letters across the back window:

IF YOUR PASSING ME YOUR SPEEDING.

This is wrong on so many levels.

Let me begin with the grammar. I'm pretty sure the writer of this message meant to say, "If you are passing me, you are speeding." The contraction of "you are" is "you're." It's really not that hard. Really.

Then there is the assumption that every time someone passes this driver it involves breaking the speed limit. I drove right past the guy because he was in the left turn lane and I was going straight. I passed him, but I wasn't speeding.

Also implied is the assertion that this driver always goes the speed limit. That's possible, but it's a strange thing to take so seriously that he felt compelled to proclaim it in large red letters across the back of his vehicle.

I'm not a bumper sticker person, let alone a three-inch red vinyl letter person, but it did make me wonder what I believed strongly enough to proclaim boldly to all the other drivers in town. Maybe it would be:

CHECK THE SPELLING OF YOUR MESSAGE BEFORE AP-PLYING THREE-INCH RED VINYL LETTERS ACROSS THE BACK OF YOUR MINI VAN.

Weight Control

I blame my mother. And why not? Isn't that how we all explain away our various phobias and addictions? She once admitted she's probably to blame for my dislike of cats. It's either that or the fact that cats are self-absorbed, boring, redundant little creatures.

I'm blaming my mother for my issues with weight control. I don't blame her for my weight problems, mind you. My propensity for carrying a little too much cushion around the middle could have just as easily come from my father's side of the family. No, I blame my mother for my preoccupation with diets.

Mom was a beautiful woman who apparently thought she needed to shed a few pounds. I confess, she wasn't svelte, but she certainly wasn't heavy. But from the time I was old enough to notice, I noticed Mom was always on some kind of diet. I can picture the little BBs she lined up on the kitchen windowsill to remind her to drink eight glasses of water a day. I remember the cartons of cottage cheese that she ate because they were low in calories (and because she genuinely liked cottage cheese, especially with a canned peach on top).

I also remember the time she told me about my father's weight loss plan. If he thought he had put on a few pounds, he'd cut out the graham crackers and milk he ate before bed. And sure enough, that brought his weight back down to where he wanted it to be. And I assume he reinstated the crackers and milk. That's so not fair.

I recently heard of a diet plan that even I am unwilling to try. It's the Dixie Cup Diet. (Don't Google it. You'll discover a very different, very gross diet plan that involves spitting out your masticated food into a Dixie Cup. There. I just told you the gross version so now you really don't have to look it up.) The Dixie Cup Diet I recently heard about is this: Eat only three Dixie Cups of food a day.

Yes, the little cups. Yes, three. Yes, a day.

It didn't matter what you ate. It could be three cups of M&Ms. But no more than three cups.

When that diet plan seemed a bit out of reach, I decided to see what was recommended for people who have diabetes. I Googled "Diabetes Diet." In addition to suggesting the eater avoid sweets, red meats, fried foods, fast foods, and a few other fatty things, the website I selected offered the following meal plan:

▶ One serving of protein (3 oz of chicken, lean beef, or fish)
▶ One serving of bread (whole grain roll, tortilla, or ½ cup pasta)
▶ One serving of dairy (cheese, milk, or low-fat sour cream)
▶ One serving of vegetables (fist sized portion or a small bowl of salad)
▶ One serving fruit (tennis ball sized or ½ cup sliced)

I interpreted the above diet plan to mean I could eat one of everything. Now that is a diet I can live with.

That's Some Glory

I heard a radio program once that invited listeners to call in and offer advice to recent graduates.

"Don't allow yourself to go into debt," offered one woman.

"Listen to your mother," said another.

Then someone said, "Get used to the idea that life is not fair."

That's a good one, I thought.

Earlier that week I'd heard three stories to prove the point.

First, a friend invited a family member to live with her, and that person ended up treating her badly.

Another friend had her home broken into and was robbed of valuable possessions and her sense of security.

Then, a friend learned that one of her family members was physically abusing another family member. The details would make you cringe.

Because I loved the people involved, these revelations weighed me down. I decided to get up early the next morning and take a long walk. I took with me the verses I'd written out to memorize. (My friend Carol and I were working on Romans 8.)

"Now if we are children, then we are heirs—heirs of God and co-heirs with Christ . . ."

I tried to understand this verse in light of the terrible things my friends were facing. *If we're children of God, shouldn't life go a little easier for us?* I reasoned.

But I read on. ". . . if indeed we suffer." *Children of God can expect to suffer?*

I read more. "The sufferings of this present time are not worthy to be compared to the glory that is to be revealed in us."

Wow—that must be some glory. If it's not worthy to be compared with our sufferings—being mistreated, being robbed, being abused—then that glory must be pretty amazing. I don't understand what that means, what that glory is, what it will look like. But I'll cling to the fact that it's going to far outweigh the worst things that happen to us in the here and now.

I returned home from my walk encouraged. I was still saddened by the hard things my friends were facing, but it helped knowing that they had the hope of something tremendous in the future.

Texting Lessons

Before sending Abby off to college, Doug and I broke down and bought her a cell phone. A room full of other things, too, mind you, but the cell phone was a pretty big deal. For years, Doug and I resisted getting our children cell phones. We just didn't think it was necessary. Our children had a million reasons why they thought they "needed" their own phones, but they failed to convince us. But then one of them said this: "I'm going away to college." Yeah, that convinced us.

As we added Abby to our cell phone plan, we also added unlimited texting. We knew that would be an important feature for Abby. So, suddenly, I had this new communication tool at my disposal.

Kate was already a pro at texting. When I first got my phone, Kate thought we had unlimited texting as part of our plan. (Doesn't everybody?) But no. We didn't even have limited texting or text-your-ten-best-friends texting. What we didn't know was that when I gave Kate permission to use my phone for what I assumed was a phone conversation, she was texting her friends. We didn't discover this until the bill came at the end of the first month. At least that bill made the regular monthly charges seem really,

really low. Really.

So anyway, after we added texting to our phone plan, Kate attempted to teach me how to text. I had a rather dated phone, and it didn't have a full keyboard. The letters were grouped together under the number keys. The number "2" had the letters "a, b," and "c." You're probably familiar with it. Even rotary phones had letters with the numbers.

There was a snazzy feature on my phone called "predictive text." The phone figured out the word I wanted when I typed in a certain combination of keys. I didn't have to painstakingly type in every letter. Kate had turned on this feature (and used it) before giving me a lesson in how to use it.

One day, shortly after getting Abby her phone, I decided to send her a text message as she headed off to go shopping. I was going to write, "Hi. Have fun."

To start the word, "Hi," I hit the "4" button where the "h" is. My smart little phone spit out the word "Hi."

Sweet! I thought. This will be really easy.

The phone automatically put in a space and waited for the next instruction. I started typing the word "have."

"H-a-" so far so good. But then it spit out a "t" giving me "hat." It automatically gave me a space and moved on to the next word. I hit "clear" and tried again. "H-a-" and again with the "t." By this time it was beeping and flashing and I decided, Okay, I'll go with "hat."

"Hat fun" is almost "have fun." I reasoned. *Abby's a smart girl. She'll figure it out.*

On to the next word. I hit the "3" key three times trying to get to the "f." But the phone thought I was asking for three letters from the "3" key. So it selected "fee—" which led it naturally to the word "feet." Again, I cleared out the word and tried again. Hitting "3-3-3" gave me "feet."

I began to giggle.

Then, sitting alone in my parked car, I started to laugh. I hit send.

"Hi. Hat feet."

Abby deftly replied, "Hat feet?"

Laughing harder, I abandoned texting and called Abby.

"Hello?" she answered.

By that time I was laughing uncontrollably, tears rolling down my face.

"Mom?"

Then Abby started to laugh, too.

I still don't text well or often. But one thing is certain—I now have a whole new way to hat feet.

This story originally appeared in *An Eclectic Collage—Creative Works by the Women of the Pixie Chicks' Writers Group*, Freundship Press, 2011. http://www.janefreund.com/freundship-press.html

FLYING CHEESE | STORIES FROM AN ORDINARY LIFE

The Trouble with Texting

I should give up texting altogether.

I trust you've read the "hat feet" fiasco. [See Texting Lessons.] Since that experience I have learned how to form coherent sentences when texting, complete with proper punctuation. Just when I thought I'd mastered the whole texting thing, I got a phone call from a Colorado Springs homicide detective.

Let me explain. That week, Abby had been taking care of some friends' cats and zucchini while said friends were out of town. I should have just trusted that she was on top of things, but I'm a mother, and sometimes I don't do so well with the whole "keep-your-nose-out-of-it" thing.

I was a little worried that our friends would come home to feline fatalities, so before settling in at the office one morning, I wrote Abby a friendly—okay, motherly—little text: Did you feed the cats yesterday?

Everything was spelled correctly; it was a full sentence, proper capitalization and punctuation—good to go. I went to select Abby's phone number. There were two very similar numbers in my "recently used" list. At one time in the past I misdialed her number and now both numbers are saved on my phone. Was Abby's number xx7-xxxx or xx9-xxxx? I know I've selected the wrong one a few times. I held my breath and selected xx9-xxxx.

Send.

A few minutes later I got a call on my cell phone. The phone number on the display screen was a little odd. It wasn't a standard seven-digit number. Maybe it's the phone company, I told myself and answered it.

"Hello?" I said.

"Hello. Is this 5xx-xxxx?" a deep voice asked, reciting my phone number precisely.

"Yes."

"This is Detective Howard with the Colorado Springs Police Department."

My mind raced. *Eric is on a camping trip—did something happen? Did someone break into the house? Has my car been stolen?*

"Yes," I responded tentatively.

"My phone number is xx9-xxxx. I've been receiving some unusual texts from this number. Can you explain this?"

Flooded with both relief and embarrassment, I began to babble. "Oh, I'm so sorry. Your phone number is one digit different than my daughter's. I texted your number by mistake. I had both numbers on my list and I wasn't sure if she was 7 or 9 and I chose 9 when I should have chosen 7. It will never happen again. I'm so sorry—"

Officer Howard chuckled. "Oh, that's a relief. I've been known to get harassing calls from people I've worked with as a homicide detective. I've had to change my number more than once."

"I'm so sorry," I continued, my heart beat back to normal. "I'll be more careful."

"Oh, don't worry about it. Now that I know it's not a disgruntled citizen it's okay. Text away."

Feeling comfortable with the friendly homicide detective I asked, "So, did you feed the cats yesterday?"

Anyway, like I said, I should just give up texting altogether. Or at least be sure of my phone numbers. In the future I'll be sure to use xx7-xxxx. Or is it xx9?

FLYING CHEESE | STORIES FROM AN ORDINARY LIFE

Goodbye, Michael Jackson

Michael Jackson's death made me sad. Not so much because I was a fan. I liked some of the earlier music by the Jackson Five, but I didn't follow Michael's solo career so much. I heard a man on the radio say that Michael Jackson's music was the sound track of his life. That does not describe me. I was touched more by the deaths of John Denver and Karen Carpenter than I was Michael Jackson. Their music did weave itself into the fabric of my teenage years.

I was saddened by Michael's death for different reasons. In a strange way I was sad because he and I were the same age. He was just two weeks older than I. So, somehow, that made it more personal. Someone my age died.

But I wasn't saddened only by the tragedy of this early death; I was saddened by the tragedy of his life. It appears he had a domineering father that robbed him of his childhood. I'm sure Michael genuinely enjoyed performing, and it sounds like he wanted to be famous. But from my humble perspective I think he should have spent a little more time riding bikes. That's what I did when I was

11. Michael Jackson was on *The Ed Sullivan Show*.

I also think his numerous cosmetic surgeries reveal an inner sadness. The day he died, Kate and I were watching some of the retrospectives on TV.

"He was a cute kid," Kate said. "Why did he get so much plastic surgery?"

"Because he wasn't happy with himself," I told her. I don't mean to imply that all plastic surgery is wrong. I've seen cases where surgery corrected some disfigurement or altered an unwanted attribute and the results were worthwhile. But was there anything wrong with Michael Jackson's face? I don't know what he saw when he looked in the mirror, but it wasn't what the rest of the world saw. The cute 11-year-old boy singing his heart out on *The Ed Sullivan Show* turned into an addicted, disfigured, and bizarre man.

And that's just sad.

The Sunday after Michael Jackson died I read these words in our church hymnal:

I'd rather have Jesus than men's applause;
I'd rather be faithful to His dear cause;
I'd rather have Jesus than worldwide fame,
I'd rather be true to His holy name.

Than to be a king of a vast domain
Or be held in sin's dread sway,
I'd rather have Jesus than anything
This world affords today.

I'd Rather Have Jesus, Rhea F. Miller, 1922.

Old Friends

One Wednesday evening not long ago, I was watching television when the doorbell rang. I turned off the TV and made my way to the front door. I opened it, and there stood a middle-aged man with a half grin on his face. He said nothing.

"May I help you?" I asked him, more than a little suspicious.

"You don't recognize me do you?" he said.

"No," I admitted, not at all comfortable with how this conversation was going.

After a slight pause, he told me his name.

Recognition overtook suspicion. He was an old friend from our days in Illinois—going back to college, in fact—someone I hadn't talked to in years. He was in town on business and decided to look us up.

"Doug," I called to my husband. "Look who's here!" I introduced our friend, assuming Doug wouldn't recognize him either.

Our friend said, "My wife and I always like it when people drop by, so I figured you'd like it, too."

To be truthful, I was self-conscious about the papers spread across the coffee table and the blanket thrown a little too casually across the couch. But our friend didn't care. So I tried very hard not to care with him.

I introduced our children—teenagers now. Then we three middle-aged friends sat and caught up with one another.

We reminisced a bit, us remembering his children as pre-schoolers running through the halls of their old house. But now he was showing us wedding pictures of those same children, cute little girls grown into beautiful brides.

Our friend was open and honest with us, recounting business failures, children who didn't believe in God anymore . . . We brought him up-to-date on us, too, though we had no real adventures to report.

"This is so great," he said, "sitting here looking at the two of you."

When he left to return to his hotel room an hour or so later, I was glad he'd gone to the effort to look us up, drive through an unfamiliar town, and ring our doorbell. I'll remember his visit next time I consider calling up an old friend. Instead of assuming he or she won't want to hear from me, I'll assume my friend will enjoy hearing from me as much as Doug and I enjoyed visiting with our old friend.

An Attitude of Gratitude

Do you need a reason to be thankful today? I can give you a few.

God tells us to be thankful. In 1 Thessalonians 5:16 to 18 it says, "Rejoice always; pray without ceasing; in everything give thanks; for this is God's will for you in Christ Jesus."

I could stop there, of course. We don't need any reason to be thankful other than the fact that it's God's desire for us to be grateful people.

To be ungrateful is to be like the ungodly. Romans 1 says people know about God because of creation. But even though they know of Him, they don't give Him the honor He's due. Verse 22 says, "For even though they knew God, they did not honor Him as God, or give thanks . . . ." Who wants to be like that?

Praise and thanks silence the enemy. Psalm 8:3 says, "From the lips of children and infants you have ordained praise because of your enemies, to silence the foe and avenger." Imagine that! We can give Satan a reason to keep his mouth shut.

If that's not enough, then be thankful because it makes you a nice person to be around. Because it can change your outlook on life. Because it feeds contentment rather than discontentment.

Be thankful simply because there is so much to be thankful for.

A Little Water, Please

I've never been great with plants. Not that we get into arguments or anything, I just tend to ignore them. And for plants, that's not a good thing. I do best with plants that thrive on neglect.

I like plants, though, and wish I were better at keeping them watered. If I remember to water them once a week they seem to do okay. But if I miss watering day, then I may not think about it for another whole week. You see the problem.

I discovered that plants seem to do well at my office. I guess it's the florescent lights. So a while back, I took one of my sad little plants to work with me. It wasn't even "Take a Plant to Work Day." It was just a mission of mercy.

I don't know what kind of plant it is. I used to think it was called a Creeping Charlie, but I've since been told that Creeping Charlie is a weed that grows in your grass. My plant is kind of vine-esque with flat, shiny leaves.

Well, most of them are shiny. I noticed recently that there was one small group of leaves in the center of the pot that were decidedly unshiny. They were downright dull. Upon closer inspection

I realized that that particular stem had become dried out where it joined the rest of the plant (no doubt due to the aforementioned "neglect" issue). It wasn't exactly dead, but it was not entirely healthy either.

I couldn't help but find a spiritual comparison. When I fail to draw daily from the Word of God, when I neglect spending time in His presence, I, too, become unshiny. Not dead, but certainly lacking in the kind of vibrant life I could have if I were better connected to the Vine. Jesus said, "I am the vine; you are the branches. If a man remains in me and I in him, he will bear much fruit; apart from me you can do nothing" (John 15:5).

I cut the unshiny stem off my plant and stuck it in some water. I'm trusting it will sprout new roots and start growing some new, shiny leaves. Maybe that's what I need to do for my times of spiritual dryness. Cut myself off from the rest of the world and saturate myself in God's Word.

Sounds refreshing.

Perspective

It's easy for me to become preoccupied with "me" and my petty little problems. When that happens, I take time to dwell on things that will improve my perspective.

Life and Death

I recently held a one-month-old baby. He was so sweet and snuggly. What else really matters? Meanwhile, I'm praying for some co-workers whose 13-year-old son is fighting cancer. For them, the battle really is between life and death. My concerns pale by comparison.

Eternity

My mother-in-law is fond of saying, "Will it matter 100 years from now?" That helps me not to get too worked up about the small stuff. What I really need to ask is, "What will matter in eternity?" That's an even more important question to answer.

Creation

When I consider your heavens,
the work of your fingers,

the moon and the stars,
which you have set in place,
what is man that you are mindful of him,
the son of man that you care for him?
(Psalm 8:3,4)

Blessings

Ask my friend Terry how he is and he'll say, "Blessed." I know he has things going on in his life that are difficult, but he chooses to focus on his blessings. I need to take a lesson from him. I have so much more to be thankful for than I have to complain about.

Sovereignty

And if I do complain, it's like telling God He's not doing a very good job at running my life. Have you seen the movie *Bruce Almighty*? I've only seen it in parts on TV, but the premise is that God gives a human the chance to run the world. In the end, the man realizes he doesn't want to do it and gives control back to God. I'm quite sure I'd come to the same conclusion in the same situation.

The Great Exchange

He made Him who knew no sin to be sin on our behalf, so that we might become the righteousness of God in Him (2 Corinthians 5:21).

When I look around me, I can see hard things happening. What I need to do is change my focus a little and see the good things, too. It's a matter of perspective.

Don't Forget the Peas

I used to think it was an Odell thing. My sisters and I are notorious for breaking into song in the middle of a conversation, as if cast in a Rodgers and Hammerstein musical. A word or phrase reminds us of a song so we'll start singing. Or at least quoting music lyrics.

Like the day I stopped at the store on my way to work. I picked up a few groceries, including frozen peas. I couldn't leave frozen peas in the car all day. They'd be pea soup by noon. So I brought them into the office and stuck them in the freezer in the kitchen.

Knowing my forgetful tendencies, I wrote myself a note and stuck it to my purse. It read, "Don't forget the peas."

Something about the meter of that sentence, and perhaps the fact that the last syllable rhymed with "eaves," made me think of an old hymn. In my mind I started singing the melody of "Bringing in the Sheaves" but the words were, "Don't forget the peas, don't forget the peas. We shall go rejoicing, don't forget the peas."

It's both a funny and annoying little quirk. It's funny at first, but by lunch I was pretty tired of The Peas song. And trust me, I didn't forget the peas after work.

Another time, Kate and I were in Safeway when I saw a bag of cracked corn. I turned to Kate and said, "Jimmy cracked corn."

"I don't care," she said, not skipping a beat.

Maybe it is hereditary.

But, as I said, I've learned it's not strictly a family characteristic. At work the other day somebody said, "Well, that's what friends are for." Of course, we all thought immediately of Dionne Warwick and friends singing those very words. Next thing you know someone Googled the lyrics and passed them along. Someone else found out who the "and friends" were (Stevie Wonder, Gladys Knight, and Elton John). Then someone looked up the song on iTunes and played 30 seconds of it. Then the boss hooked up his iPod to some speakers and played the song for all to hear. Yes, he had "That's What Friends Are For" on his iPod. Doesn't everybody?

It's fun sharing music and memories. When we all know the same song, it's like discovering we have a mutual friend.

Then there's the whole movie line quotation thing, but I won't get into that. I'll just let it be.

Remodeled

Sometimes I wish things wouldn't change.

I recently saw a photograph of the Iowa farmhouse my Aunt Betty and Uncle Bill lived in when I was growing up. Back then, it was a simple, two-story brick house, with an insanely steep staircase going from the main floor to the bedrooms above.

The house sat across the road from the cornfields my uncle farmed with my grandfather. A pair of binoculars sat in the living room windowsill so we could track Uncle Bill and Grandpa in their day's work, or watch the storms coming in, at times welcomed, at times not.

There was a porch with a swing in the front, and an enclosed porch on one side next to the kitchen. I loved that house.

But in time, Aunt Betty and Uncle Bill needed a place without an insane staircase, and they moved into town.

A few weeks ago, one of my sisters traveled through Iowa and she drove by Uncle Bill and Aunt Betty's old house, stopped the car, and snapped a photograph.

When I saw the photo I was shocked—and a little horrified. The new residents added a whole wing onto the old farmhouse. In fact, it's like two houses, joined with a window-lined passageway. Very modern. Lovely. But wrong.

I liked it the way it was. With the porch and the swing.

And Aunt Betty and Uncle Bill.

And that's the point, really. I miss knowing Aunt Betty is bustling around kitchen making Rice Krispie Treats. I miss seeing Uncle Bill on his tractor, or rubbing the head of his favorite dog.

The remodeled house is just another reminder that time is marching on, that nothing stays the same. Except our unchanging, eternal God. And that's where I need to place my hope and my joy. Yes, houses come and go. Even the people we love come and go. But Jesus? The same yesterday, today, and forever.

A Matter of
Life and Death

Once, when my daughter Kate asked about my day at work, I told her, "It was pretty good, until the end of the day."

I explained that I was in a meeting and someone told the story of a young woman in another country who had been killed by her father and brother because she decided to leave the family's religion and follow Jesus. There are other details to the story that I can't share publicly, details that brought the story close to home. Some mistakes had been made that compromised this woman's safety, mistakes that I could have made as easily as anyone.

The thought of this young woman losing her life left me stunned and almost unable to concentrate on the rest of the meeting.

"We have it so easy here," Kate said.

She's right, of course. Believers in the United States are not usually tortured for following Jesus. Some people are shunned by their family. I was not. Some of us might experience teasing. I have, but just a little. Discrimination on the job? I've only worked for Christian organizations so I've never been passed over for a promotion because I was a Christian. I've had it easy. Maybe too easy.

What have I sacrificed for following Jesus? Virtually nothing. I asked myself some hard questions that night. I didn't want this young woman's life and death to pass by my consciousness without changing me somehow. If nothing else, I want to live more courageously. I want to be more bold in declaring that I am a follower of Jesus. It is a truth worth dying for. And a truth worth living for.

Scattered Thoughts from a Busy Week

It's wonderful to have friends that understand without me having to explain everything.

Skype is fun. We set it up at home and talked to Doug's sister and her husband as our test drive.

I'm not a huge cake fan, but I shared an enormous piece of chocolate cake from a restaurant with Kate and Eric that was served with fresh fruit and raspberry sauce. Of that, I am a fan.

A friend of mine just gave birth to a beautiful ten pound baby boy. My beautiful baby boy weighed 9 lbs 13 1/2 oz. I'm a little upset that she beat me.

Everybody has troubles. Everybody.

The other night I was making gumbo while my husband and our three teenagers played *Monopoly* on the dining room table. In that moment, all was right with the world.

In the grocery store, I thanked a soldier for serving our country.

I'm going to do that more often.

I'm getting very gray.

I don't know what the future holds but I know who holds the future. That's a little trite but I like it.

Birds. I'm delighted to hear them singing in the spring, but I know I will come to curse them for disturbing my sleep some summer morning. I shouldn't do that.

I miss my parents.

Barber's *Adagio for Strings*. It makes me cry every time.

I'd love to have a typewriter. (But not in place of a computer.)

You don't have to be old to be grown up.

You can be old and not very grown up.

I love citrus "flavored" lotion.

Whenever I don't know what to do, I refer to these verses: "Rejoice always, pray continually, give thanks in all circumstances; for this is God's will for you in Christ Jesus" (1 Thessalonians 5:16-18).

"Oh, That's Okay"

Squeak, squeak, scrape.

That's the sound of me pushing my soap box across the floor. I'm about to step up and give you an ear full. Be warned.

"I'm sorry."

These two words cause me a lot of anguish. But it's not what you might think.

It's not that I find it difficult to apologize (or that I find it easy). It's not that I think anybody owes me an apology. It's that our society doesn't really know what to do with those two little words.

First of all, we quite often use "I'm sorry" when we really mean "I apologize." The phrase "I'm sorry" means "to be filled with sorrow." For example, it's a common practice to say "I'm sorry" to someone who has just experienced the loss of a loved one. You're letting that person know that you are filled with sorrow over his or her loss. You're not apologizing for anything.

I doubt that I'll be able to get the entire English speaking world to say "I apologize" when that is what they mean rather than "I'm sorry." And I can't say it's wrong to use "I'm sorry" in this way. I'm sure I do it myself. But it would be more accurate and more clear to use "I apologize" when that is what we're really trying to say.

What bothers me even more is that our society doesn't know how to respond to an apology. Let me give you a for instance.

After a recent shopping trip, a friend of mine discovered her four-year-old daughter came home with a candy bar that had not been paid for. After confirming the suspicion that the candy was hijacked from the store, and after a conversation about the fact that stealing is wrong, my friend returned to the store with her daughter so the little darlin' could confess to the manager what she'd done and ask for forgiveness.

With a little help from Mom, the sweetie told the store manager she'd stolen a candy bar.

"I'm sorry," the child humbly confessed.

"Oh, that's okay," the manager responded.

My friend wanted to strangle the shopkeeper (though that would have required more apologizing so she refrained). "Don't tell her it's okay," my friend wanted to say. "It's not okay!"

I was equally appalled. We the people need to learn how to say "I forgive you." That's the proper response to an apology (provided you're willing to extend forgiveness). Or perhaps "I accept your apology." Or at the very least, "Thank you for the apology." And sometimes it's appropriate to say, "That's so nice of you, but I don't feel like an apology is necessary." Anything but "that's okay." If it were okay, there would be no need to apologize!

Please, people. Formulate a good response of your own, practice it privately if you must, but don't say "It's okay." That's not okay.

Squeak, squeak, scrape.

Happy Tears

I remember the day I shed a few tears on a morning bike ride. It wasn't because of the wind in my face, though there was some of that. It wasn't the pain building up in my knees, though there was some of that. It wasn't even the Cujo dog that tried to take me down, though there was some of that. (Note to leash owners: The leash device works best when one end is fastened to the dog's collar. Waving the leash menacingly at the dog is not the preferred use of the device.) No, I shed a few tears because I was thinking about my daughter Kate.

Kate had graduated from high school a few days before. That morning, as I pedaled along, I remembered how cute she looked in her white cap and gown, her blue eyes shining, her curly brown hair cascading from beneath the universally awkward graduation cap.

I remembered her poise as she crossed the stage, pausing briefly to shake hands with her principal and other school dignitaries. She didn't even trip in her snazzy red heels, purchased especially for the occasion.

As I rode along, my mind went back to when Kate was about

three years old. We were at one of our favorite parks (the one with the merry-go-round) and I was sitting on a blanket downhill from the playground. Suddenly she left the sandy swing area and started down the hill to me. She spread her arms wide, broke into a huge smile, and aimed herself toward me. Her legs could hardly keep up with the momentum pulling her down the hill. But she stayed upright, and fell into my waiting arms.

"Lord," I prayed, "help me never to forget this moment." And I never have.

Kate brought us many hugs and smiles during her first 17 years. And it made me tear up a bit thinking about it that morning.

That fall she headed off to college to study chemistry, 700 miles away. I knew I'd miss her terribly. But I was excited for her, too. She was so ready for the next phase of life, running full steam ahead, arms wide open, headed into her future, bright, hopeful, smiling.

Stories from the ER

One of my friends works in a local emergency room. Every once in a while she will pass along a story about some strange case she encountered—usually involving a lot of blood. But today I heard about a 20-year-old patient who died and whose parents chose to donate 17 organs and other tissues from their child's body to many sick, suffering strangers.

I don't know what 17 things were donated beyond some of the obvious ones—eyes, kidneys, heart. During the surgery there were 17 nurses on hand to receive a particular body part for a needy recipient. My friend observed that each of the people transferring a body part to its destination paused to thank the donor before leaving the room.

Can you picture it? I'm sure each person knew the urgency of handling the donated item quickly. But they acknowledged that each organ had come at the cost of a human life.

My mind went quickly to Jesus. He died so that I might know life. His back bled, His joints popped, His eyes closed, His heart stopped. For me. For you. For the world He loved.

So I pause . . . *Thank you, Jesus. Thank you, Jesus. Thank you, Jesus.*

FLYING CHEESE | STORIES FROM AN ORDINARY LIFE

It Was a Trying, Difficult, Frustrating, Faith-Building Week

I hope you've read the classic children's book *Alexander and the Terrible, Horrible, No Good, Very Bad Day* by Judith Viorst. I hope you've read it because it's a tremendous book. But I also hope you've read it because it will make you appreciate the kind of week I had.

On Monday, Abby and I were rear-ended in the van. It was the other driver's fault, but the other driver was not going to drive our van to the body shop for estimates. I would have to do that. And when would I find time to do that? I could tell it was going to be a difficult week.

The next day my neck hurt when I turned my head to the left.

Then, on Wednesday, I went downtown for a lunch meeting. I parked the car on the street. I didn't know it at the time, but someone went all rock 'em sock 'em on our bumper. Nobody left a note. Nobody took responsibility. We'd have to pay for the repairs.

I could tell it was going to be a difficult week. I think I'll move to San Diego.

On Saturday, the transmission in the van went out. We couldn't drive in reverse. Not only would I have to take the van to a body shop for an estimate but now I'd have to take it to the mechanic for repairs. And find another way to get around. I wonder if I could find a way to get to San Diego.

On Sunday the furnace freaked out. It blew cold air. And the fan ran on and on. We turned it off. The house got cold. I bet it's not cold in San Diego.

The next Monday I drove the van to the body shop for an estimate. On the way there I couldn't go faster than 30 mph. The transmission was getting worse. I decided not to drive the van to San Diego.

Then my cell phone died. Not ran-out-of-battery-died, but dead died. It really isn't too surprising. It was practically an antique. But still. I was without a phone. And I'm pretty sure I gave my upgrade to one of my offspring.

This all came at a time when our bank account showed the effects of helping two daughters pay for college. So why did God choose this week to have both vehicles damaged, the transmission fail in the van, the furnace die, and my cell phone give out? It seemed like an obvious question. Even for someone in San Diego.

I told my pastor about our string of unfortunate events. He said he was sorry it had been a difficult week. He said I should trust God. He said God was working for my good and His glory. Hmm, not a "poor Becky" in there anywhere. So I decided to trust God.

My friend Randy loaned me his car. His new car. A cute little Mazda stick shift. I had great fun driving it around for a few days. And I realized I had wonderful friends that were willing to trust me with valuable possessions and inconvenience themselves for my benefit. Randy's Mazda gave us a way to get around while the van was in the shop.

The transmission in the van had been replaced a year ago so it was still under warrantee. It was repaired at no cost to us.

The furnace repair man came and flipped a small red switch hidden inside the furnace. We paid only $85. The house was soon as toasty as San Diego.

Then, a couple days later, as Doug drove the car home from work, a man pulled up next to him and motioned for him to roll down his window.

"I can pull those dents out for you," he said. He suggested he and Doug pull into a parking lot to talk. "Most body shops will tell you to replace the entire bumper or the entire side panel," he said. And he's right. That's what we'd been told. "I'll pull out those dents and you'll just have a little scratch in the paint." Doug got his number.

That same night I went to the AT&T store. I didn't have an upgrade on my phone. But Doug did. So I used his upgrade and got a groovy new phone with a full keyboard. Only $20 after rebate.

How 'bout that? My good and God's glory. And I didn't even have to move to San Diego.

Branded

In recent years, my job in organizational communications has allowed me to learn a little bit about "branding." Simply put, a company's brand is its identity. The idea comes from the branding done on cattle ranches. As you're probably aware, each ranch has a unique symbol that they burn into the hide of every cow on the farm with an iron "stamp," or brand. The "Double D Ranch," for example, might have a brand of two "Ds." If a Double D cow wanders off, other ranchers know where that cow rightfully belongs because of the two Ds burned into its hide.

The idea is similar in corporate branding. There are certain things that identify a company—a logo, colors, slogans. These help create an identity for an organization. But my boss is quick to point out that branding is not just about logos and color palettes. It's about experience. People should have a uniform experience whenever they encounter a particular organization. Whether you patronize a company in Boise or Boston, you should have the same experience.

One of the most successful brands in existence is *Coca-Cola*. With some slight modifications, Coke tastes the same across the world. The classic red and white swish is identifiable from Argentina to Austria.

I read recently that after The Coca-Cola Company had been bottling their product for a while, they decided they wanted a unique bottle, something that would be identified as a Coke bottle even if it were shattered against a wall. And they succeeded. The shape, the color, the texture—everything about that bottle says "Coke."

Now imagine having all this branding business in mind and reading this verse:

" . . . I bear on my body the brand-marks of Jesus" (Galatians 6:17).

While commentators offer different interpretations of what the apostle Paul might have meant here, the most obvious meaning is that Paul was referring to the many scars he carried from being repeatedly beaten and scourged. His body was literally scarred because of his association with Jesus.

But the word "brand-mark" is also the word used when slaves of that century were branded—like we brand cows today—with a mark burned into their skin that identified that slave as belonging to a particular person.

The word "brand-mark" is powerful enough when it's taken to mean Paul's physical scars. It's even more profound when you consider that Paul may have had a double meaning in mind—that he was a slave of Jesus Christ and bore His brand. But I can't help but expand the application still more as I consider some of the present-day meanings associated with the word "brand." I ask myself—

Do I clearly identify myself with Jesus?

Do people have the same experience whenever they encounter me? Am I consistently Christ-like?

If I were to be thrown against a wall and broken into a million pieces, would people look at those pieces and see Jesus?

Oh! to be like Thee, blessed Redeemer,
This is my constant longing and prayer;
Gladly I'll forfeit all of earth's treasures,
Jesus, Thy perfect likeness to wear.

Oh! to be like Thee, oh! to be like Thee,
Blessed Redeemer, pure as Thou art;
Come in Thy sweetness, come in Thy fullness;
Stamp Thine own image deep on my heart.

Oh! to Be Like Thee, Thomas O. Chisholm, pub. 1897

Thank You, Dr. Olney

CBS Sunday Morning is one of my favorite television shows. I say that even though I rarely watch it. The program airs Sunday mornings (obviously), and because I habitually attend church Sunday mornings, I hardly ever see it.

(I know, I could record it, but that would require me to be organized. However, I recently discovered I can watch it online.)

What I love about this show is that it tells human interest stories. It's not "hard news"; it's people. It may inform, it may inspire, but it does so by telling someone's story.

I recently watched a story about a doctor, Richard Olney, who spent decades treating and researching ALS (*Amyotrophic lateral sclerosis,* commonly known as Lou Gehrig's Disease) only to be stricken with the disease himself in his late fifties.

As his speech faculties began to fail, he recorded his voice on his laptop saying phrases that he thought would be useful to him. He could click a button on his computer and it would broadcast his voice saying, "Good morning," "Thanks for stopping by," or "I have a speech problem."

He also recorded a message for his wife: "I love you, Paula."

It prompted me to wonder, "What phrases would I record if I knew I would lose the ability to speak?"

"I love you" is a good start.

"I'm sorry."

"I'm proud of you."

"I understand."

"Sing me a song, please."

"See ya later."

"Don't worry about it."

"How may I pray for you?"

On the heels of this mental exercise, I read Luke 6:45: "The good man brings good things out of the good stored up in his heart, and the evil man brings evil things out of the evil stored up in his heart. For out of the overflow of his heart his mouth speaks."

The words I speak are formed in my heart. So I'd better be sure my heart is filled with good things. Things like gratitude, kindness, compassion . . . . Philippians 4:8 says, "Finally, brothers, whatever is true, whatever is noble, whatever is right, whatever is pure, whatever is lovely, whatever is admirable—if anything is excellent or praiseworthy—think about such things."

Dr. Olney passed away in 2012. I hope I can learn from his story and chose my words carefully while I still can. Better yet, make right, excellent, and admirable words a natural overflow of what is in my heart.

My Old Friend, *The Sound of Music*

I had an unpleasant illness one spring (are there pleasant illnesses?) that prompted me to spend an unusual number of hours in bed. Between naps, I watched TV and a couple of favorite movies. One of them was 1965's *The Sound of Music*. It took me two days to get through the three-hour musical, but I enjoyed it, again.

Each time I watch it I'm struck by the same things:

Julie Andrews' voice. Such expression, such effortlessness. I recently researched her life journey and learned that her step-father discovered her four-octave range when she was eight years old. Most of us can sing two octaves; many trained singers can cover three. She described it as "freakish," calling it "an adult voice in a little body." Sadly, vocal cord surgery in 1997 forever altered her clear soprano.

The Alps. The mountains aren't just a beautiful setting, they're an important character. Without the Alps, there are no "hills" to be alive with the sound of music. *Climb Every Mountain* becomes a less meaningful analogy. And the movie would lack its dramatic conclusion—the escape by foot over the mountains.

The Nuns. I'd love to sing in a multi-part ensemble like that, singing lowest alto. One of the nuns, Sister Sophia, is played by none other than Marni Nixon. Who is Marni Nixon, you may ask. She's the talented singer that dubbed the singing voices of several notable film actresses of the day. She sang for Deborah Kerr in *The King and I*, Natalie Wood in *West Side Story*, Audrey Hepburn in *My Fair Lady*. In the DVD commentary for *The Sound of Music*, director Robert Wise comments that audiences were finally able to see the woman whose voice they knew so well.

My favorite line. A Nazi sympathizer, Herr Zeller, attends a party at the Von Trapp home. In a tense conversation about Hitler's suspected invasion into peaceful Austria, the Captain says to Herr Zeller, "If the Nazis take over Austria, you will be the entire trumpet section."

Zeller responds, "You flatter me."

And then, the Captain says my favorite line in the movie: "Oh, how clumsy of me. I meant to accuse you."

So polished, so dignified, but so cutting.

Liesl is pretty, but pitchy. The dear soul was flat most of the time. If I can hear it, couldn't the musical directors? Why didn't they re-record her parts until she got it right? That really bugs me.

Which child is my age? I've always wondered which of the children is closest in age to me, so I finally looked it up on the Internet. I'm the same age—a month younger—as the littlest girl, Gretl, played by Kym Karath (born August 4, 1958). Somehow fitting, since I'm the youngest child in my family of five girls.

It's nice to have a few movies I can watch again and again "when I'm feeling bad." They're like old friends that know just what to say to make me feel better, to help me "sing once more."

Step Out of the Traffic

I recently read an interesting article called, "Want To Be More Creative? Get Bored."

The author talked about the value of being bored, of having time to let your mind process problems, time to "do" nothing and just let your brain work.

He said, "I'm not referring to killing time on your smartphone, your iPad, or your laptop. I'm not even talking about paging through a book. I mean bored as in doing absolutely nothing."

His "bored" time is his daily swim.

"As I power up and down the lanes, I rethink what I've learned. I now have the time and space to solve whatever problems have arisen. It's an important meeting with myself, and I keep it religiously. Because the day I lose it, I've lost myself."

I've noticed this same phenomenon, but rather than "bored" I'd call it "quiet." I can remember times when quiet produced some great ideas—things to write about, ways to solve a relationship problem, or even a new way to handle the clutter in my house.

But my world is rarely quiet. And I'm entirely to blame. I turn on the TV when I'm getting ready for work. I play the radio in the car. I turn on music when I'm cooking. Why is that? What am I so afraid of?

The only time I listen to the quiet is when I take a walk. I don't have an mp3 player to take music with me wherever I go. But I dislike quiet so much that I sometimes take a book along and read while I walk. It's a skill I've mastered over the years because I don't like the "do nothing" feeling I get when I'm walking. I also dislike waiting without something to do. Maybe I need counseling.

God understands the need for quiet. Psalm 46:10 says, "Be still and know that I am God." *(King James Version).* Look how it's worded in other versions of the Bible:

"Cease striving and know that I am God" *(New American Standard).*

"Let be and be still, and know (recognize and understand) that I am God" *(Amplified).*

"Step out of the traffic! Take a long, loving look at me, your High God." *(The Message).*

So now what? Do I promise to create some quiet, "boring" space in my life? I don't want to make promises I can't keep. But I tell ya what: I'll try. But keep it quiet.

---

http://www.fastcompany.com/1829462/martin-lindstrom-buyology-marketing-branding-creative-thinking-creative-pause?partner=homepage_newsletter

Yep, That
Sounds Like Me

My name is Becky, and I'm a Pharisee.

They say admitting your problem is the first step to recovery, right? So I admit it. I'm a Pharisee.

I credit my pastor with bringing me to this confession. In his sermon one Sunday, he suggested we all might have a little Pharisee in us. I had to admit, I have more than a little.

Pharisees were a group of religious leaders in Jesus' day who were known for their legalistic adherence to Jewish law. As my pastor said, "The Pharisees focused on externals. Pleasing God meant following a list of do's and don'ts."

Yeah, that sounds like me.

He went on to say, "The Pharisees viewed themselves as the standard of spirituality. They were spiritually proud."

The more Pastor talked, the more I heard myself in his words.

I was very "Pharisee" when it came to my reaction to the death of Whitney Houston in 2012. I heard people refer to her as a follower of Jesus and I thought, "Really? A drug abuser?"

I did catch myself—"Yes, Becky, Jesus followers can fall victim to addictions." But that didn't stop my self-righteous, legalistic, internal tirade. As images and interviews of Ms. Houston flooded the television I'd think, "Did you see that dress? Did you hear the words of that song? How can she be a Christian and use that language?"

Growing up, I learned to define Christianity as a list of do's and don'ts. I understood that my relationship with God was based on my faith in Jesus, but from there I added things like—

"Good Christians don't go to movies."

"Good Christians don't play cards."

"Good Christians don't dance."

"Good Christians don't swear."

And the list could go on and on. And so, my friends, that makes me a Pharisee.

But I want to change. I want to stop expecting people to live up to my vain standards. Stop expecting Christians to dress a certain way, talk a certain way, live a certain way. I want to invite the possibility that people like Whitney Houston may know more about faith and the grace of God than I ever will.

To Envy Robert Frost

While at the library with Eric one day, I saw a CD with the title, "The Voice of the Poet: Robert Frost." I'd always enjoyed Mr. Frost's poetry, so I thought it would be fun to hear him read his own work. I checked it out and took it home.

The recordings were made later in his life. His voice warbled a bit. That, and his New England accent, reminded me of Katherine Hepburn. He read simply, evenly, sometimes too quickly, I thought, with less drama or emotion than I expected.

I realized again why I like his poetry. He wrote about ordinary things: birch trees, owls, apple picking. He discovered the poetry of simple conversations, of a leaf covered path, the grass.

Dust of Snow
> *The way of a crow*
> *Shook down on me*
> *The dust of snow*
> *From a hemlock tree*

Has given my heart
A change of mood
And saved some part
Of a day I had rued.
(Robert Frost, 1923)

I found myself envious of his talent. But as I read the brief biography accompanying the recording I learned his life was filled with tragedy. His father died when he was 11 years old. His first son died of cholera at age four. His sister was institutionalized.

If his tragic life somehow birthed his genius, then I'll pass. I'll remain content with my simple prose and keep my mostly happy life.

Anonymity

I'll never win a Pulitzer,
Though Robert Frost won four.
My prize—a happy family;
I'll want for nothing more.
(Rebecca K. Grosenbach, 2009)

Made in the USA
Charleston, SC
24 April 2013